The Blessing

WORKBOOK

The Blessing

WORKBOOK

Gary Smalley and John Trent, Ph.D.

A
JANET
THOMA
BOOK

THOMAS NELSON PUBLISHERS
NASHVILLE

Acknowledgments

The authors would like to thank Janet Thoma, Susan Salmon Trotman, and Laurie Clark. Special thanks to 'Leen Polinger for her tireless efforts and hard work.

Published in Nashville, Tennessee, by Thomas Nelson, Inc., and distributed in Canada by Word Communications, Ltd., Richmond, British Columbia, and in the United Kingdom by Word (UK), Ltd., Milton Keynes, England.
Unless otherwise noted, Scripture quotations are from the HOLY BIBLE: NEW INTERNATIONAL VERSION ®. Copyright © 1973, 1978, 1984 by International Bible Society. Used by permission of Zondervan Publishing House. All rights reserved.
Scripture quotations noted NASB are from the NEW AMERICAN STANDARD BIBLE. Copyright © 1960, 1962, 1963, 1968, 1971, 1972, 1973, 1975, 1977 by The Lockman Foundation and are used by permission.
ISBN: 0-8407-4555-9
Printed in the United States of America
1 2 3 4 5 6 — 98 97 96 95 94 93

Contents

PART THREE: RECEIVING THE BLESSING AS AN ADULT

Part One

UNDERSTANDING THE BLESSING

The Journey toward the Blessing

Diane shook her head in disbelief. Her mind refused to accept what she'd heard. "Tell me exactly what my son said."

Her father-in-law replied, "We were talking about what day you'd return and how glad the two of you would be to see him. His little eyes looked down and he said, 'Dad will be glad to see me . . . but Mom won't. *She doesn't love me.*'"

Diane couldn't believe her eight-year-old son Jerry felt that way. If anything, she was afraid she loved him *too* much. She shared the problem with her husband, Don, and he suggested they read *The Blessing*.

Shortly after they had gone through the book together, Diane went into her son's room to pray with him one night. She asked, "Honey, do you know what I really like about you?"

Without hesitation, Jerry said, "*Sure . . . nothing.*"

Perhaps you are like Diane—you love your child or children dearly, but don't seem to be able to convince them you care. Perhaps it's your spouse or friend or parents who need your affirmation.

Perhaps you are like Jerry—even as an adult, you honestly believe one or both parents don't, or didn't, love you. Possibly they didn't: They were abusive, critical, had too-high expectations, or even abandoned you. It's possible that they, like Diane, simply didn't know how to express the love and acceptance necessary for you to feel loved and accepted.

Whether you've missed out on the blessing or need to learn to give it to those around you, this workbook is a tool for you to use to walk toward wholeness and positive relationships. The exercises are designed to help you learn and use the steps of the blessing, to provide the blessing to others, and to find the blessing for yourself.

Working through the workbook will take time, commitment, persistence, and perhaps some soul-searching. But, if you master these principles, you'll find the effort well worthwhile. Diane did.

When her son, Jerry, admitted he couldn't think of anything about himself that she loved, Diane choked back tears. She said the first positive thing that popped into her mind, "Sweetheart, I do love the way you have such a good imagination and are able to make up such neat stories. I like that in your Daddy, too."

After that first night, Diane mentioned something she liked about Jerry every day. It became almost a ritual at bedtime. She reported, "Within months, he was sitting on my knee again and letting me kiss him goodnight. It was overwhelming to see him become a child again."

For nearly eight months, Diane had the joy of winning back her son's love and affection, and then it happened: every mother's worst nightmare. While Jerry was delivering papers on his bicycle only a few blocks from their home, he was struck by a drunk driver and killed instantly.

In the midst of her grief, Diane brushed away tears and said, "I look back over those months preceding his death and thank God over and over that I was able to see my mistakes. God was gracious in giving me those special months. Jerry died knowing I loved him. I thank God for that."*

You, too, may want to praise God for what you learn in this workbook as relationships with your family and friends grow.

In addition to strengthening or rebuilding family relationships and producing a sense of self-worth in children, the blessing also helps ensure closer, happier social ties with others as the children grow up.

In a thirty-six-year study reported in the April *Journal of Personality and Social Psychology*, psychologists Carol Franz, David C. McClelland, and Joel Weinberg found that children who receive physical affection and warmth are apt to have closer marriages and friendships, better mental health, and greater work success.

Affection from Dad is as influential and lasting as affection from Mom, according to the study. But warm affection from both parents is most likely to result in a well-adjusted adult with a strong sense of internal security.

Completing the exercises and assignments in this workbook will help you give your children, spouse, friends, and others this advantage.

HOW TO USE THIS WORKBOOK

First, commit yourself to learning to give the blessing and to completing all the exercises in the workbook. Complete the blanks in the contract on page 6.

Most people achieve such a commitment by setting a specific time and place to work. You might choose to work half an hour a day, five days a week, or an hour or two one day a week. Determine the time that fits best into your schedule and keep it clear to work on *The Blessing Workbook*. Be realistic when you put down the

*Diane's story, like all the stories in this workbook, is taken from actual events. The names and some of the geographical details have been changed to protect privacy without altering the content of the event.

BELIEVING that being able to give the Blessing will enhance not only the lives of my children, spouse, and friends but also my life, I, (your name) _____ _____, agree to complete the exercises, assignments, and readings in *The Blessing Workbook.*

My goal is to complete the workbook by (date) _____. In order to do this, I will set aside (hours) _____ each week to work on the workbook. I will work not just to complete the tasks, but to make blessing others an integral part of my life.

I will be accountable to (name of friend, relative, other caring person, or study group) _____, to whom I will report my progress on a regular basis.

IN WITNESS WHEREOF, I set my hand on this (day) _____ of (month) _____, 19_____.

_____
(Your signature)

amount of time you know you can free up for this project. Speed is not as important as achieving your goal of being able to give the blessing.

What day and time is best for you? (Example: Tuesday through Saturday from 6:00 to 6:30 A.M. or Friday from 2:30 to 4:00 P.M.)

Day (or days): _____

Time of day: _____

Choose a place where you'll be uninterrupted, comfortable, and quiet—a site where you feel free to laugh, to cry, to think.

The place you will work: _____

Find a safe place to keep your workbook. You'll feel more comfortable writing your answers if you know no one will read what you write unless you offer it.

Start at the beginning of the workbook and work through each chapter, each step, until you reach the end. Begin each session with prayer, and complete each exercise thoughtfully. The act of writing an answer isn't important: arriving at the truth is. The exercises have been designed to lead you step by step . . . to your goal.

You named one person in your contract to whom you would report your progress. When that person is also working through *The Blessing Workbook,* you both gain more than if only one participates. Working with a support or counseling or study group is another possibility. Whether you work with one person or a group, you will be able to discuss your findings and feelings to get the most out of what you are learning.

If you are working alone, choose someone who will care about your progress and listen to your reports. Diane went through *The Blessing* with her husband. Perhaps your spouse is your best choice. Perhaps a close friend will be most helpful to you if you're not married.

If you are working in a group, list the members' names.

_____ _____

_____ _____

_____ _____

As you begin your journey toward the blessing, we want to give you our blessing. Without knowing who you are, we know you are special in God's eyes. He cares for you, and we care too. We know that, if you diligently give yourself to learning and practicing the steps in this workbook, you will become a person of blessing.

2

The Need for the Blessing

In the Azores, it is common for a younger person to greet an older relative with the phrase, "Bless me, my uncle [or aunt or father, and so on]." The uncle responds, "I bless you, Sally. Do you have a particular problem?"

If Sally does have a problem, she can lay it on her uncle's shoulders and he can give her assurance, advice, or affirmation. Sally's request for a blessing may just be a request for affirmation—Sally's need to feel her older relative's acceptance.

We all long to be accepted by others. While we may say out loud, "I don't care what other people think about me," on the inside we all yearn for intimacy and affection. This yearning is especially important in our relationship with our parents. Gaining or missing out on parental approval has a tremendous effect on us, even if it has been years since we have had any regular contact with them.

LACKING THE BLESSING

In Chapter 1, we mentioned the study showing that children who received affirmation from at least one parent were more apt to have closer marriages and friendships, better mental health, and more work success. That same study showed the opposite to be true of children who didn't receive warmth and affection from their parents. These children will more likely lack personal acceptance, which in turn leads to difficulty in making decisions and relating well to people.

Without the blessing, some people carry a huge reservoir of unreleased anger that eventually explodes and spreads hurt over everyone around.

Others are bound by a paralyzing fear that keeps them from functioning at their full capacity—fear of what people think, fear of failure, fear of rejection, fear of not measuring up, fear of fear itself.

Pessimism, another result of missing the blessing, actually threatens life. Peterson and Bossio, in their book *Health and Optimism* established a medical link between a patient's optimism or pessimism and his or her health.

Their examination of study after study on cancer patients revealed the destructive potential of pessimism.[1]

People who have never heard affirming words or who were never encouraged often lack communication skills. In a study reported in *USA Today,* 92 percent of people turned down for a job or a promotion were not turned down due to lack of job skill, but to lack of communication skills.[2]

The lack of the blessing often has devastating effects in every area of our lives and at all stages of our lives.

Everyone needs to receive the blessing.

Rachel didn't. Now in her mid-50s, Rachel will not invite friends for coffee or lunch. Her self-esteem is so low that she would rather be lonely than risk their saying no and thus feeling rejected.

While she was growing up, Rachel believed that her mother favored her younger brother. Instead of affirming Rachel's value, her mother taught her to stay in the background and consider everyone else better and more important. Rachel never felt cherished. As a result, she failed to find the blessing, and her sense of inferiority became so strong that no amount of affirmation has been able to change her negative self-perception.

Geoffrey can't remember either of his parents ever saying "I love you" or giving him a hug or a pat on the back. They met his physical needs, but he never felt they gave him the blessing. In rebellion, he did the opposite of what his parents wanted. He tried to hurt them as deeply as he was hurt. Today, thirty years after his parents' death, he still yearns for that acceptance he never felt as a boy, and he grieves over the damage his anger caused them all.

Betsy reacted to missing the blessing in yet another way. Nothing she did seemed good enough. If she got an A, only an A+ was acceptable; if she won a part in the school play, she felt bad that she didn't get the starring role; if she made the team, she wondered why she wasn't captain. In an effort to please, she always tried harder. Acceptance was always just out of reach.

As an adult, Betsy's striving evolved into a common American quality: workaholism. She often worked twelve- to sixteen-hour days, six and seven days a week, in order to gain approval. She projected her need to please her parents onto her work situation and her employer. Regardless of how many accolades she received as a result of her work, she never felt she quite made the grade.

Others who miss the blessing may struggle vainly to sustain or attain close relationships—with a spouse, children, friends, or even with their heavenly Father.

FAMILY SNAPSHOTS

Take a look at your family by filling in the names of your parents and grandparents on the diagram below. This may look complicated, but it's really quite manageable. Called a "genogram," this is simply a tool to allow you to see the dynamics of a family that can affect you and future generations.

Do it step by step. Write in the names of your brothers and sisters in birth order. Add boxes if necessary.

If there were other important people in your life—an aunt, a teacher, a neighbor—put their names in the boxes marked OSP (other significant people).

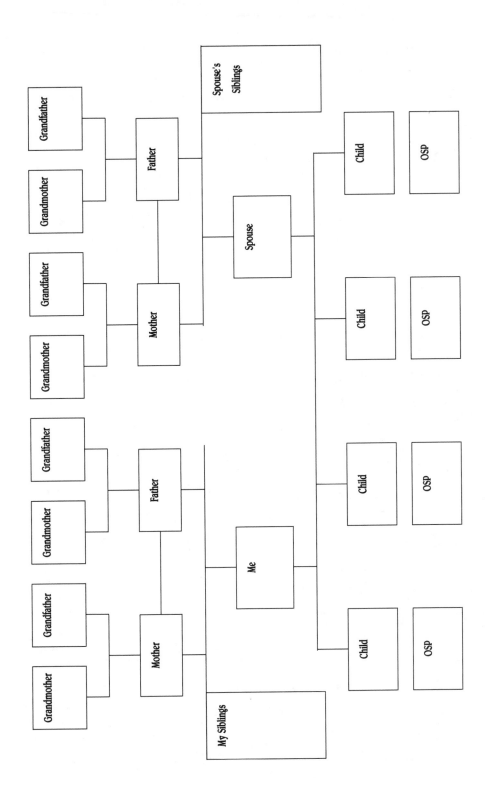

Put a check by the names of the people who lived in your home when you were a child.

Describe your family when you were six or eight years old. To help you get started, think back to a typical mealtime. Who was there? What was the conversation about? What was the atmosphere (happy, at odds, silent)? _____

_____

_____

_____

_____

_____

_____

Now look at individual family members.

Do you feel that your father generally approved or disapproved of you? _____

What did he like about you? _____

_____

_____

_____

What did he dislike? _____

_____

_____

_____

How did he show approval or disapproval? _____

_____

_____

_____

How did you feel about your father when you were a child?

_____

_____

_____

_____

When you were a teen? _____

_____

_____

_____

_____

As an adult? _____

_____

_____

_____

Did your mother generally approve or disapprove of you?

_____

What did she like about you? _____

_____

_____

_____

What did she dislike? _____

_____

_____

_____

_____

How did she show approval or disapproval? _____

_____

_____

_____

How did you feel about your mother when you were a child?

_____

_____

_____

_____

When you were a teen? _____

_____

_____

_____

As an adult? _____

_____

_____

_____

Describe the relationship you had with your brothers and sisters
when you were a child. _____

_____

_____

_____

_____

_____

_____

What is your current relationship with your siblings?

_____

_____

_____

_____

_____

Did you feel another child was favored above yourself? _____
If your answer is yes, what made you think so? _____

_____

_____

_____

_____

How did what you perceived as favoritism affect your relationship with that sibling? _____

_____

_____

_____

_____

How did it affect the relationship between you and the parent
who showed favoritism? _____

_____

_____

_____

Record how other significant people, if any, affected your life.

_____

_____

_____

_____

_____

What is your perception of yourself today? Are you successful? A failure? Happy? Depressed? Yearning? All "together" emotionally?

_____

_____

_____

To help understand your current relationships, examine your family groupings as you were growing up. The space within the square below represents the whole of your universe. The figure in the center is you; write your name on it. Use stick figures, draw in and name the other members of your family as they related to you in your earliest memories of family life.

Did Dad dominate? Make him a little bigger and put him at the top. If Mom was submissive, but you felt she was in close relationship to Dad, draw her somewhat smaller, a little lower, but close to Dad. Was Mom the driving force? Put her higher. Were Mom and Dad repressed? Affectionate? Touching? Or far away?

Where were each of the kids—close to Dad? Mom? You? Each other? Away from everyone?

Were certain family members always close, bonded together? Connect them with a solid line (_____). Were there family members who were sometimes close and sometimes distant? Connect them with a broken line (_ _ _ _ _ _).

If one of the children acted as part-time or substitute parent, draw a circle around him or her and tell how you felt about him or her. _____

_____

_____

_____

_____

If there were other significant people in your family, put them in place. To whom did you confide your doubts, rejoice over triumphs, reveal your deepest feelings? _____

_____

_____

_____

_____

Think about how your placement of family members in the square reveals family relationships. Did you put anyone completely out of your universe—outside the square—because they were emotionally or physically beyond your emotional reach? Were you closely clustered or widely spread? _____

_____

_____

_____

_____

_____

_____

If your family grouping changed drastically (due to a move, loss of job, birth, divorce, remarriage, or death) when you were growing up, draw another universe and show the new relationships.

Describe the extent to which you received affirmation from your family. _____

_____

_____

_____

_____

_____

_____

Did it come from one parent? _____ Which one? _____
Both? _____ Neither? _____ Another significant person? _____
Record how that person affirmed you. _____

_____

_____

_____

_____

If you feel neither parent blessed you, write how you would have liked them to behave. _____

_____

_____

_____

_____

_____

We'll look at how the presence or absence of the blessing affects our relationships in a later chapter.

Now, we'll take a close look at the blessing itself.

3

The Blessing

Whata is this "blessing," this important act that no one can live well without?

Here's one way to explain it: "words and actions that provide an indelible picture of affirmation in a person's mind and memory." To bless is to honor, praise, salute. To be blessed is to be given power for success, prosperity, and longevity.

THE BLESSING

Blessing began with God. Highlight the words of blessing in each of the following verses:

"So God created man in his own image, in the image of God he created him; male and female he created them. God blessed them" (Gen. 1:27–28).

"Then God blessed Noah and his sons, saying to them, 'Be fruitful and increase in number and fill the earth'" (Gen. 9:1).

"I will make you into a great nation and I will bless you;/I will make your name great, and you will be a blessing" (Gen. 12:2).

"After Abraham's death, God blessed his son Isaac" (Gen. 25:11).

"Then the man said, 'Let me go, for it is daybreak.' But Jacob replied, 'I will not let you go unless you bless me'. . . . Then he blessed him there" (Gen. 32:26–29).

God still blesses people today. He has "blessed us in the heavenly realms with every spiritual blessing in Christ" (Eph. 1:3).

Following God's example, Hebrew families developed a tradition of blessing their children. Though linked to the birthright, the blessing was somewhat different. The birthright was intended primarily for the firstborn child, but a specific, personalized blessing was given to each child in the family. Isaac had a separate blessing for Esau. Jacob blessed each of his twelve sons as well as two grandsons.

The Hebrew blessing became a rite of passage—the milestone marker between childhood and adulthood. This blessing rite is still practiced in Orthodox Jewish homes today. As a rite of passage, a blessing is important, whether it signifies passage from childhood to adulthood or an affirmation at birth or marriage or death.

It is crucial to adapt the five-step pattern of the blessing from the Old Testament into a daily assurance of worth and acceptance for our children, spouse, family, and friends. Though we are presenting the steps one by one, all five are required to give a blessing.

A blessing is powerful. In Old Testament thought, it could surround a person with God's protection. It was given any time a person was going beyond sight, over the horizon. Normally, a parental blessing was irrevocable. It kept on giving throughout the child's life.

Though a curse was a major catastrophe, *it could be removed by the stronger power of a blessing.* This idea is important to remember as you begin to deal with your memories and hurts of the past.

When God blessed, nothing could intervene. In Numbers 22, when Balak attempted to bribe Balaam to curse the Israelites, we learn that "you must not put a curse on those people, because they are blessed" (v. 12). In Numbers 23, God said through Balaam, "How can I curse those whom God has not cursed?/How can I denounce those whom the Lord has not denounced?/. . . I have received a command to bless;/he has blessed, and I cannot change it" (Num. 23:8, 20). God has the final say on our blessing.

We can give our children, spouse, parents, or friends the benefits of daily blessing. It doesn't have to be a big production; it can be something simple. How often have you done the following things?

_____ Really listened when others talk
_____ Let a child spend a day with you at work
_____ Admitted you make mistakes
_____ Left a plate of cookies with an "I love you" note
_____ Used any one of hundreds of other ways of saying, "You're special; I care."

Parents can bless children, spouse can bless spouse, friend can bless friend, child can bless parent, church workers can bless their members. It only takes a knowledge of how to do it, the desire, and a commitment to express love and caring.

Recall one specific instance in which you received your parents' or your spouse's or a friend's blessing. _____

_____

_____

_____

_____

_____

In our book *The Blessing,* we explored five elements necessary to giving a blessing, as given in the Old Testament. These five elements, or steps, were

- Giving meaningful touch
- Speaking words of blessing
- Expressing high value
- Picturing a special future
- Making an active commitment to seeing the blessing come to pass

In this workbook, we will look at these steps in-depth, as well as three other steps that are an essential part of the process:

- Evaluating the blessing
- Learning to live without the blessing
- Receiving God's blessing

Let's take a brief look at each of these steps now to get acquainted.

EVALUATING THE BLESSING

In order to give the blessing, you must first receive the blessing. Evaluating your personality type and the types of those who reared you will help you understand why you may have missed the blessing. Evaluating the personality types of those you love will also help you in bestowing the blessing upon them.

Mary Jane remembers her mother as a fun-loving, encouraging woman. She was Mary Jane's number-one fan. When Mary Jane played in a volleyball tournament in high school, her mother was there. When Mary Jane was in a school play, her mother was there. Her mother frequently took her out to the movies or to go shopping. They were good friends.

Mary Jane's mother could show her daughter affection and could motivate her to keep going when times got tough. But she had a hard time disciplining Mary Jane. As a result, Mary Jane was often frustrated, trying to find boundaries she could not exceed. She entered college a spoiled young woman, with little regard for the feelings of others. When Mary Jane finally began to understand her mother's personality, she was able to accept the good she had received from her mother and discipline herself.

Consider the personalities of the people who raised you. What one characteristic of each of these people do you recall? _____

_____

_____

Name a specific incident where this characteristic was evident to you and how you were affected by it? _____

_____

_____

Did this characteristic help give you the blessing, or did it contribute to your missing the blessing? _____

We will explore four different personality types in Chapter 5, and consider how each of these personality types responds when the blessing has not been received.

STEP 1—MEANINGFUL TOUCH

Before even a word is spoken, the blessing is conveyed by touch. One five-year-old told her mother she loved the way Janice tousled the top of her head when she walked by. "It makes me feel special."

Touch played a part in biblical examples of blessing. In Genesis 48, Jacob blessed Ephraim and Manasseh by putting his hands on their heads. The act of touch communicates warmth, affirmation— even physical health.

Touch also conveys acceptance. A hand on the shoulder, an arm curled round in a hug, a kiss, can say, "You're all right. I care."

Max found this out when he was forty-five and near death after a major heart attack. He'd grown up knowing his dad loved him—not from anything that was said, only by the look in his dad's eyes. His father, a German farmer, was raised in such a way that he could never bring himself to say "I love you" or otherwise verbalize the love he felt.

When Max was an adult, he left the farm and moved to California, where he was when he had the heart attack. Warned that Max might not survive, his wife called the family.

Max's dad flew all the way across the country to be with his son. When he arrived, he came to his son's room in the ICU unit where he was hooked up to various tubes and monitoring equipment.

Max told us that day on the radio that he had never, even once heard his father verbally tell him, "I love you." He knew his father did love him, but he had always longed to hear those words of blessing.

"But that day," Max told us, "My father did something where I know now for a fact that I did get his blessing."

"What was that?" we asked, our interest sky-high.

"He simply pulled up a chair and sat next to me . . . and held my hand for about an hour."

And while we were both touched by his story, that's when he dropped the bombshell.

"And if you think that's something, let me tell you the rest of the story," Max continued.

"Three days after my father flew cross-country to be at my bedside, *he died.*"

"Today, I thank God for my heart attack, because if it had never happened, I wouldn't have known for a fact that I had my father's blessing like I know now."

Give an example from your life of how a touch showed you love, lifted your spirits, made you feel better, encouraged you, or added a sparkle to your day.

_____

_____

_____

_____

_____

If you asked your children, spouse, or a friend what particular touch from you meant most to them, what do you think they'd say?

_____

_____

_____

_____

Ask your children, spouse, or friend to answer the above question. What do they say? _____

_____

_____

_____

_____

_____

STEP 2—SPOKEN WORDS

Touch, however important, can't carry the whole load. A verbal message of acceptance, appreciation, or encouragement is the next step in giving the blessing.

When Jacob blessed Manasseh and Ephraim, he not only laid his hands on their heads, he also said, "In your name will Israel pronounce this blessing:/'May God make you like Ephraim and Manasseh'" (Gen. 48:20).

With words, we can express acceptance and love, both vital to emotional health and well-being, or we can express rejection and degradation.

As an example, Denise grew up in a home where her father saw to it that she received every element of the blessing. He encouraged her, went to her sports activities and school open houses, and supported her every way he could.

One of the most supportive memories for Denise was his pet name for her: *Angel Darling.* He even made up a little song that used her pet name and told of his love. The last time she heard the song was just before her father died. He asked her to sit on the edge of his bed, gave her a hug, and sang the Angel Darling song to his "little girl."

Denise said, "It was hurtful and healing at the same time. I hurt because I knew it was the last time I'd ever hear him sing my song, but it meant so much to me. It was Dad's way of saying, "You're special and I've always loved you."

Donna grew up in just the opposite kind of home. Donna's father provided one of the most degrading homes imaginable. Donna was tall and slender, stunningly attractive, but when I (John) met her she refused to dress in any color but black. In part, her color choice came from the darkness she carried inside from hearing the nickname her father called her each day, *Demon Daughter*. Donna lived a miserable life until she met Christ and He freed her from the title her father had bestowed.

Think back to your growing years and the words people said to you. What words of acceptance or encouragement do you remember? _____

_____

_____

_____

_____

What effect did they have on you? _____

_____

_____

_____

_____

Did you hear words of degradation, as Donna did? Give an example. _____

_____

_____

_____

_____

What words of encouragement or discouragement do you say to those you should bless? _____

_____

_____

_____

_____

_____

_____

_____

What effect do you think your words have on those people?

_____

_____

_____

_____

_____

STEP 3—EXPRESSING HIGH VALUE

To be effective, our words and actions must express our esteem for the one we're blessing and affirm that this person is valuable. In the Scriptures, recognition is based on who a person is, not on his or her performance.

In Jacob's blessing of Ephraim and Manasseh, he said, "May they be called by my name and the names of my fathers Abraham and Isaac . . ." (Gen 48:16). Their value lay not in anything they had done, but in who they were—sons of his son, now to be reckoned as his sons to receive the blessing God gave to Abraham.

We can say or do a wide variety of things to attach high value to another person. To which of the following acts do you attach high value?

_____ Praising thoughtfulness
_____ Acknowledging good qualities or character traits
_____ Rewarding good performance
_____ A pat on the shoulder for an obedient attitude
_____ A note in the lunch bag saying, "You're tops."

Which one of the acts above is based on what someone does rather than who he or she is? _____ How do you suppose these words make a person feel? _____

_____

_____

_____

Another way to express high value is by our presence, as Alex discovered. I (John) met Alex on a plane recently, and we fell into conversation. When Alex learned that I worked with families, he asked for advice. His son was a leading player in Little League in terms of home runs, extra base hits—a good member of the team, but a goof-off in the dugout.

The father said, "Tell me if I did something wrong. My wife thinks I did. She's really upset with me."

"What happened?"

"We were at the game, and Joe, my son, was messing around, so I pulled him over and said, 'Listen. Either you get serious, in the dugout as well as on the ball field, or I'm leaving.'"

His son shaped up for a while, but soon began to clown around again. Sure enough, the father yelled at his son and stormed out, and missed his son's big playoff game, including seeing him strike out in the last inning and lose the game.

That father told me, "I think I did what he deserved. But my wife is sure I did the wrong thing. _What's your opinion?_"

Instead of responding, I asked, "Did your dad ever do something like that to you?"

Instantly, Alex hung his head. "All the time. My dad used to motivate me by his absence. He withdrew himself to punish me. *He still does*. If he comes to visit and I do something that displeases him, he'll up and leave." Here is a father who could attach high value to his son with his presence, and chooses not to.

To you, and to me sitting next to him on the plane that night, it was obvious that this man was carrying a negative pattern from one generation to the next. When tension built and the going got tough, he would take off instead of staying in there with his son.

This father not only missed the game, he missed an opportunity to comfort his son and say, "I love you anyway. It's OK. I'm still proud of you." He could have reversed a negative pattern and become a father who could attach value to his son with his presence and a few words: "Hey, I'm here to work for you. I'm staying because you're important to me."

How did a significant person in your life let you know he or she valued you highly? _____

_____

_____

_____

_____

Give an example of how you show your children, spouse, family, or friends that you value them. _____

_____

_____

_____

_____

_____

_____

_____

STEP 4—PICTURING A SPECIAL FUTURE

Well-meaning but ill-informed parents try to motivate their children with negative statements. Too many children hear, "If you don't (whatever), you'll never amount to anything," or "Hey, dum-dum, what went wrong this time?"

What other put-downs have you heard people say, either to you or to someone else?

_____

_____

_____

_____

_____

_____

_____

_____

What do you think would be a more effective way of trying to spur those we bless to better achievement? _____

_____

_____

_____

_____

_____

We can give those we bless a sense of security and confidence by conveying that the gifts and character traits they have right now are attributes that God can bless and use in the future.

If we look back at our example with Jacob blessing Manasseh and Ephraim, we see that he pictured a marvelous future: they would be held up as examples of being blessed by God. He also included God's blessing of their becoming great nations.

The positive/negative message about one's future can be given without words, as in the case with Mike and Doug. Mike had marked musical talent and had made all-state choir. On the afternoon of Mike's performance of the year, his brother Doug had a soccer practice. Not a game, a play-off, or a championship game, just a routine practice.

Mike's dad, who had been a pro athlete, chose to go to the soccer game rather than the choir presentation. His decision told Mike, "What you're interested in, what you want to be, the talent you have, who you are isn't important to me."

If you had been Mike, how would you have felt? _____

_____

_____

_____

_____

_____

Mike struggled all his life to feel accepted by others because of this incident and many more indications that music wasn't as important as sports. He could never feel that what he accomplished had any merit.

How do you suppose Doug felt? _____

_____

_____

_____

_____

Did you have a similar experience? _____

_____

_____

_____

_____

How did it make you feel? _____

_____

_____

_____

What has the long-term effect been on your life? _____

_____

_____

_____

_____

Did your parents or other significant persons do or say anything to assure you of your capability to have a bright future? _____

_____

_____

_____

_____

In what ways are you copying your parents as you bless or withhold the blessing from others? _____

_____

_____

_____

_____

STEP 5—AN ACTIVE COMMITMENT

This element is a "kicker." It requires sticking with the program even when your child misbehaves or the person you're blessing disappoints you—and you're ready to toss up your hands in despair. It's committing time and energy to involvement in that person's life to see that the words of blessing you speak come to pass.

Words alone, even words of high value picturing a special future combined with touch, cannot completely communicate the blessing. A commitment to carry out the blessing is essential. Everyone intent on giving the blessing needs to rely on the Lord to give them strength and staying power to confirm their children's, spouse's or friend's blessing.

Jane was a young adult who missed the blessing. As a result, she had become so shattered she couldn't relate to anyone. She withdrew emotionally until her parents were unable to deal with her. Finally, she was taken into a home for treatment. Stan and Amy, new Christians, were chosen to work with Jane. They determined to visit her and tell her of their love and of Jesus' love for her.

The first day, they entered her room and said hello. Jane looked at them through lackluster eyes, picked up her chair, turned it to face the wall, and sat down with her back to them.

Stan and Amy looked at each other and drew a quick breath of prayer. Amy said, "We just came to tell you we love you. If there's anything we can do for you, we want to do it."

Stan echoed, "Yes. We love you. We want to help you."

The next day, they returned. Again Jane picked up her chair, turned it toward the wall, and sat down. Again Stan and Amy told her they loved her and added that Jesus loved her too. The next day was the same, and the next, and the next.

In fact, daily for months, Stan and Amy kept their commitment to bless Jane. Jane sat facing the wall. When they tried to touch her shoulder, she huddled into herself and ducked her head. Despite discouragement, Stan and Amy kept their commitment and went on visiting Jane.

Finally, one day *almost a year* from the first time they saw her, when they entered the room, Jane looked at them, nodded briefly, and sat facing them. Feeling as if they'd achieved a major victory, Stan and Amy told her again of their love and Jesus' love. It wasn't long until Jane was talking and even letting them hug her when they left.

In what ways can you remember your parents, spouse, or another significant person actively working as Stan and Amy did to see that you got their blessing? _____

_____

_____

_____

_____

_____

_____

_____

LEARNING TO LIVE WITHOUT THE BLESSING

Even as you are making an active commitment to carry out the blessing in other people's lives, you may have to learn to live without the blessing from certain individuals. Learning to live without the blessing frees us to be all God would have us be, loving others without demanding that they fill a gap perhaps left by those with whom we grew up.

Understanding our parents' backgrounds, forgiving them, and learning to honor them are key factors in being able to live without the blessing. It is possible, as we will see in Chapter 18 of this workbook, to learn to live without the blessing even if your parents are not living.

RECEIVING GOD'S FAMILY BLESSING

The final step in the process of giving and receiving the blessing is receiving God's family blessing. The only way to enjoy the blessing fully is through a relationship with Jesus Christ. God can provide a blessing you may have missed. But even if you have received the perfect parental blessing, it is not complete without the blessing of God.

The family of God can also bless us.

These eight ingredients of the blessing—evaluating the blessing, giving meaningful touch, speaking words, expressing high value to the one being blessed, picturing a special future for him or her, confirming the blessing by an active commitment, learning to live without the blessing, and receiving God's blessing—enables personal acceptance to thrive and bloom in our homes and lives.

The diagram below represents what we've learned about the blessing. Write one aspect of the blessing in each box. Then list one or two examples of how these elements can be expressed.

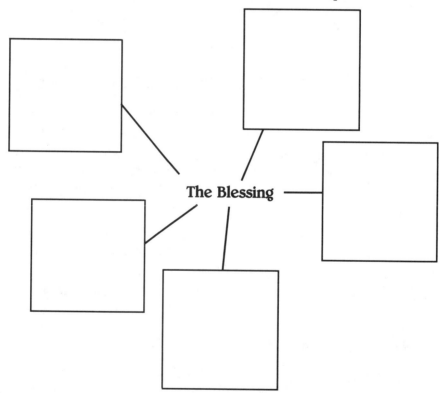

Unfortunately, not all families follow this pattern. In the next chapter, we'll look at homes that withhold the blessing.

4

Homes That Withhold the Blessing

Many people read "self-help" books and see themselves in the examples given. They think, "No *wonder* I'm the way I am. I had dreadful parents and a dysfunctional home." Some will overreact and even put down good parents who tried their best. But the fact remains, of the people you'll see today, five to six out of ten will have missed out on their parents' blessing. A large segment of our population grew up in homes that withheld the blessing.

The purpose of discussing these homes is not to give grounds to blame parents or guardians. In fact, the opposite is true. Studying truthfully and honestly about these homes and patterns can lead you to *honor* your parents and take responsibility for how you behave today.

In a later chapter, you will discover ways to feel compassion for your parents. You may find answers to some difficult questions that have been bothering you. Right now, however, let's examine homes that withhold the blessing.

NINE HOMES THAT WITHHOLD THE BLESSING

You won't necessarily find yourself, your parents, your children, or your friends in each or every or perhaps any of these homes.

You may recognize how you missed the blessing, or realize that you are withholding the blessing from your children in the same way. You may see and understand why your spouse or parents or friends feel the way they do. We pray that, in seeing, you'll begin the healing process.

Living for years within a family leaves a profound mark on every family member. If that mark was constructive, the child does well. If it was destructive and isn't dealt with and forgiven, that child will almost always leave the same harmful mark on his or her own children. People who choose to carry around anger, self-pity, and resentment chain themselves to the past and are likely to repeat it.

Often, parents who withhold the blessing lack the knowledge or skill to pass on the blessing. They don't lack love, only the means of showing it. Others do lack love, and their actions can deeply scar their children. When those children reach adulthood, they spend years struggling to free themselves from their past and seldom feel free to enjoy a commitment relationship in the present.

As you read through the symptoms of each home, put a check mark in the title box if you relate to that home or know of someone who grew up in such a home.

☐ *Home One—Favoritism: Facing Flood or Drought*

In this home, one child is favored over the others. One gets a flood of blessing; the others suffer drought.

Ted was the oldest of five brothers. While they were growing up, Ted was the only one their father cared about. Dad took Ted fishing, spent time with him, kept up on his activities, gave him all the blessing. He gave none to the four younger brothers.

After their father died, Ted decided to right things by blessing his brothers. *They totally rejected him.* If he sends birthday or Christmas cards, they're returned unopened. If he calls, they hang up. The father's favoritism drove a wedge of resentment between Ted and his brothers that Ted has been unable to remove.

In a home that shows favoritism, none of the children come out winners. Obviously, those experiencing drought miss the blessing and feel anger and resentment as they watch it splash over the favorite. They yearn for a drop of attention.

The favorite child is also in a precarious position. Like Ted, he or she can experience problems in trying to build relationships with siblings. Others with most-favored status suffer guilt and defensiveness about receiving the blessing at high cost to others. They may feel that they are not receiving a blessing at all, only a counterfeit—designed to fill the needs of the parent or guardian rather than the child.

Favoritism can be shown in a variety of ways. It can be exclusive partisanship as in the family above. In another family we know, the grandmother, who lived in the home, showed her bias by asking the favored child do all the "little helper" tasks. Some parents heap material gifts on one child because they feel guilty for loving another child more. One mother admitted she was stricter and more demanding of a favorite child. In whatever guise it takes, favoritism cripples the child and withholds the blessing.

☐ *Home Two—The Home with Overcontrol*

Many people who missed the blessing try to establish a regimented life—to make everything and everyone work to please them—on their schedule. They want to maintain a status quo.

However, life is unpredictable. Good health can fail, people can lose long-term jobs, get pregnant again after an "operation" to prevent it, or get transferred across country. Every time the unpredictable happens, the overcontroller tries to force others into a preconceived pattern.

Margaret's mother is an overcontroller. She keeps Margaret toeing her mark with comments such as, "I want you to stop right now and think of what it will be like when I'm lying in my casket and you are at my funeral. I want you to imagine sitting there and remembering what an ungrateful, uncaring daughter you were."

The picture is so graphic that Margaret always does whatever her mother wants, to the detriment of her relationships with her husband and children. Several months ago, Margaret and her husband were at a weekend marriage relationship conference. Saturday morning, Margaret got an emergency call that her mother had fallen and needed her help.

Margaret abandoned her husband at the conference and rushed to her mother's home only to discover that her mother's fall was minor, that nothing was wrong.

People like Margaret, who are victims of overcontrol, almost always let themselves be overcontrolled because of the threat held over them. They find early in life that it's not safe to confront or defy, so they grow up feeling they never can break free. They may react in one of three ways.

1. They give in and let the overcontroller destroy all other relationships, as Margaret was doing with her mother.

2. They become helpless, because the overcontroller keeps them from learning independence and responsibility, leaving no room for personal growth. They lose initiative and motivation.

3. They become depressed. Because they're unable to confront or be assertive (that's too dangerous), the anger they feel toward the overcontroller turns inward and becomes depression. (A very helpful book on controlling people is Tim Kimmel's *Friendly Fire* (Colorado Springs: Focus on the Family, 1993.)

☐ *Home Three—The Blessing Just Out of Reach*

Jim never measured up. He couldn't plow a furrow straight enough to please his father. He couldn't work hard enough or long enough. In an effort to find something he could do well enough to gain his father's approval, he joined the army.

It was 1969, and joining the army for Jim meant going to Vietnam. He'd been in the country less than a week when he was severely wounded in an ambush. His "million-dollar" wounds were severe enough to be sent home and to get him an honorable discharge. Jim went to his Dad's farm to recuperate.

One day, as he was helping his dad on the farm, he walked over to where his dad and three other men were talking. One of the farmers told him respectfully. "Jim, we're really proud of you. You fought well for your country and are glad to see your wounds are healing OK."

Jim's father snorted. *"Don't be proud of my son.* He probably got shot running away from the enemy."

At that moment, Jim realized he would never be able to do anything to satisfy his dad. He was right. His dad never did bless him.

Like Jim, many children spend their lives seeking acceptance because they never quite measured up. The standards, set so high, left not even a possibility of attaining the goal the parent demanded.

Most children who grow up in this type of home will be lured into a futile chase for their parents' blessing. In reaching for parental acceptance, they often become workaholics.

☐ *Home Four—The Punishing Personality*

There are two types of homes with punishing personalities. One punishes by silence.

Art's dad was like that. He refused to talk with anyone at the dinner table. As a small boy, Art used to sit with tears in his eyes wondering, "What have I done to make Daddy this way?" He felt punished by his father's silence. Silence communicates a negative message: "I'm here, but you can never come to me."

The other punishing personality home is one with either abuse or anger. Angie's home was a typical example.

When Angie was in high school, she was asked to be an attendant at a friend's wedding. On the day of the wedding, excited and full of anticipation, she bathed and put on her bridesmaid dress. She was just ready to step out the door when her father, drunk and angry, intercepted her. "Where do you think you're going?"

"Well, Daddy, I'm going to Nancy's wedding. I told you about it."

Daddy threw his drink at her, splashing most of it on the beautiful dress. She mopped it up as best she could, but she arrived at the wedding smelling like a brewery. The happy occasion turned into an embarrassing and hurtful experience for Angie.

☐ *Home Five—Blessing Exchanged for a Burden*

In this home, a terrible transaction takes place. A child is coaxed by guilt or fear into giving up all rights to his or her goals and desires. Instead of living his or her own life, the child does what the parent demands. In return, the child gets a blessing that lasts until the next time the parent manipulates him or her to fulfill the parent's desires.

If the child never breaks free, he loses his identity and spends his life enslaved to following what his parent demands.

Bob's parents owned an auto supply store and expected Bob to take over the business when Dad retired. So, instead of going to college, Bob went to work at the store. He got a lot of practical on-the-job experience, but he never had enough time off to get the education he wanted. He kept his father's blessing as long as he worked at the store.

Bob started attending a church and accepted Christ as his Savior. As the months dragged on, he began to feel that God had a specific call on his life to go into the ministry. He volunteered to work on the youth staff at the church and felt he'd found his life's work.

One night, as they were closing the store, Bob said, "Dad, I've been thinking. I know you want me to take over the store, but I feel I need to go to Bible school so I can become a minister. I'd like to cut back and only work part-time."

His father banged his fist on the counter and yelled, "The store's not good enough for you, huh? Well, I'll show you. You don't have to work. Not at all. You're fired."

Bob's father not only sacked Bob, but he found a replacement—someone who wanted the store. He not only shut Bob out, he refused to help Bob in any way, financially or give him the blessing.

Bob's father would bless him only as long as Bob carried the burden of running the store. Bob worked his own way through Bible college and seminary. It took a lot longer than if his father had helped, but he escaped the home that exchanged a blessing for a burden.

Parents who hold out the elements of the blessing to their children with such strings attached—for Bob it was the store; for others it's showing up every week for Sunday dinner or babysitting the younger kids—do them a grave disservice.

A blessing is a gift that is given, not something that needs to be earned. Like God's love, it is an act of unmerited favor and unconditional acceptance bestowed upon a person of high value.

☐ *Home Six—Treading Through Emotional Mine Fields*

Emotional mine fields are often found in the homes of alcoholics. For example, Nick comes home from school and heads for the refrigerator, thirsty for a drink of milk. He grabs the milk carton and drinks right out of it. His dad stands there watching; no problem. The next day, Nick does exactly the same thing, and his dad comes unglued. Nick gets pulverized.

Nick never knows from one minute to the next what will set off the fireworks. He never knows when or where the explosion is coming from.

Emotional mine fields create fear and distrust. The Bible tells us that "There is no fear in love. But perfect love drives out fear" (1 John 4:18). The reverse is also true. Fear has the capacity to drive out love, so the more fear you have, the less loving you'll be.

See what happened to Andy when he was ten. Andy came home from school one afternoon and, leaving his chores undone, went out to play with his friends. Later, he saw his dad drive up and loped home to greet him and have dinner. He ran up to his dad's car, eager to say hello.

Dad opened the door, stepped out of the car, and, without a word, swung a fist at him and knocked him out. Moments later, Andy came to, and his dad jerked him up and yelled at him for not doing his chores. Andy didn't know that he had really upset his mom, who had called his dad and complained. "That was almost 30 years ago," Andy told me (John). "But I can still remember how my jaw hurt.

That's an emotional mine field. Andy doesn't know what's going to happen the next time he walks up to the car or the next time he sees his dad. When is the next punch coming? When will he upset his mom again and get decked?

☐ *Home Seven—Unyielding Family Traditions*

Homes that wave the banner "Unyielding Traditions Live Here" do not consider right and wrong—only tradition. In Bob's family, the oldest son for generations has been a minister or a doctor or a lawyer, so Bob's oldest son is expected to be one too. No one in Martha's family has ever married outside his or her social class, so Martha's daughters are expected to follow the tradition. If Janet doesn't pledge the right sorority, her mother will withhold the blessing.

Parents reject or emotionally abandon their children if they fail to carry out the family tradition. The parents know full well the impact of their punitive decision to withhold their blessing—and that's exactly why they do it. Their expectations have been dashed, their pride hurt. They want their son or daughter to hurt as well.

These parents can sit through sermon after sermon about forgiveness, never once misunderstanding what the pastor says, and still refuse to give the son or daughter who broke tradition a blessing.

Children who miss the blessing because they broke an iron-clad family tradition often feel emotionally bankrupt. Once their decision was made and carried out, there was no way to please their parents and restore the blessing.

☐ *Home Eight—Keeping Family Secrets*

Family secrets are meant to "protect" everyone in the home. If no outsider knows that Uncle George committed suicide or Sister

Suzie had an abortion or Cousin Earl was born in the poor house or Great Grandpa rode with the Plummer gang, the family is safe.

But in keeping the secret, Sister Suzie may well be missing out on the blessing, and Uncle George certainly did. If the family secret is that Mom's an alcoholic, then not only are Mom, Dad, and the kids apt to miss the blessing, but Mom's well-being is jeopardized.

Sometimes a family secret is kept from a particular family member—the case in Ralph's home. Ralph had invited his father, now elderly and ill, to live with him and his wife. Not long after his father moved in, Ralph lost his job. Ralph and his wife decided it would be best not to worry his father, so they instructed the kids not to tell.

Every morning, Ralph got up, showered, and left just as if he were going to work. Many days he job hunted, sometimes spending the time in the library, but he always returned home at the same time in the evening.

It wasn't long until Ralph's father's health deteriorated. Ralph took his dad to the doctor, who examined him and said, "You know, there's something else going on. Something besides a physical ailment."

"Yeah," said Dad. "I don't know what it is, but something's wrong with my son. It's eating me alive, tearing me up inside. I can't sleep at night."

The doctor called Ralph in from the waiting room and said, "Let's have it out. What's going on that's bothering your father so much?"

Ralph looked at his dad, drew a deep breath, and said, "I lost my job. I didn't want you to worry, so I couldn't tell you."

His dad interrupted. "Lost your job? That's wonderful. I thought something was really wrong. Gee, I lost my job when I was your age. I remember it was tough for a while, but we made it. Why didn't you tell me, son? I could help."

This family secret kept Ralph from the blessing of being comforted by his father.

Keeping family secrets doesn't decrease tension, it increases it—not only for the ones outside the secret, but also for those trying to keep it.

☐ *Home Nine—Receiving Only Part of the Blessing*

In this final home, a child receives the blessing, but only in part. There are several ways in which this can happen, and each has the power to leave a child feeling only half-blessed.

Three common situations in which a part of the blessing can be withheld are divorce, desertion, and adoption.

Divorce

In a typical divorce, the mother has custody of the children and the father has visitation rights. Early on, the father lavishes attention on the children, but as the months go by, contact begins to decrease. By the time three years have passed, many fathers see their children once a month or less.

As the visits decrease in frequency and duration, the children increasingly feel angry and insecure.

Danny was eleven when his parents divorced and his dad moved out. That last night, he clung to his dad, begging him to stay.

"It's all right, Danny. Nothing's going to change. I'm going to be right there for you, go to your games, help with homework—just like now."

Dad kept his word, for a while. Not only that, but he brought expensive presents, took Danny to movies, and did all kinds of things with him—some he'd never done before. Mom, living on a shoestring budget, couldn't compete with the largesse that her husband provided, and Danny felt resentment at her practical demands.

Seven months after the divorce, Danny's dad quit coming so often, and the gifts stopped. He was now living with the woman he'd left Danny's mom for and becoming more and more involved with her two children. He no longer kept his word that "nothing would change."

Danny lost his father once when he moved out. He lost him again when he no longer had time to make the extra effort to see Danny. Children of divorce usually suffer this double loss.

The blessing a father gives his child is as important as the blessing of the mother. When it is absent, there is a vacuum in the child's life that needs to be filled.

When One Parent Deserts the Family

Desertion by a parent can be harder on a child than losing him or her to death. When a parent dies, a child knows that in this life the opportunity to regain a missing part of the blessing from that parent is gone. When a parent deserts his or her children, they know that "out there somewhere" is a living person who still has the power to bless.

Gene's father left one day when Gene was about three years old. He just walked out and never returned. For a while, his mom frantically looked for his dad, wondering if he'd been in an accident or hurt in some way. But she didn't find him. Gene cried himself to sleep many nights, wondering if he'd done something terribly wrong to cause his dad not to come home.

Many years later, when Gene was an adult and working as a salesman for a farm machine company, he attended a national sales meeting. One of the other salesmen walked up to him and said, "Yours is an unusual last name. A guy who lives on our block in Atlanta has the same name. Any relation?"

Gene didn't know, but he asked a few questions and the next day decided to call and talk to the man. After a bit of preliminary conversation, Gene said, "You know, I think I'm your son. I'd like to reestablish contact. I'd love to introduce you to my family.

His father replied, "I left for a reason—I didn't want any part of you or anyone else in your mother's family. I'm not interested in seeing you, and I don't want you to call any more."

Gene was devastated *all over again*. That lifelong hope that sometime, somewhere, he'd find his father and get the blessing died.

Most cases of desertion leave the same unanswered questions: Is the person all right? Is he dead? Is there a problem? Am *I* the problem? And, far too often, if contact is made, the one who deserted has no inclination to restore any communication.

Dealing with Questions Raised by Adoption

Yet another group of children commonly struggle with gaining only part of the blessing. These are adopted children who ask, "Why did my natural parents leave me?" The question comes up even in the best of homes where a child is totally secure in his or her adoptive parents' love.

Many feel compelled to seek their natural parents in an attempt to regain that part of the blessing they lost. Adoptive parents can provide about ninety-five percent of a missing blessing for that adoptive child, but there is still five percent that cannot be filled by adoptive parents, no matter how much they love the child.

That five percent may be filled if the child and the birth parents are reunited and the birth parent gives the blessing. If that never happens, the five percent can also be filled by a relationship with Jesus Christ.

YOUR HOME

As you read through the various homes that withhold the blessing, you checked those to which you related in one way or another: your home, your spouse's home, your parent's home, a friend's home.

The following questions relate to each home. Complete the questions only for those homes that have meaning in your life at this time. The persons involved could be parents, guardians, spouses, siblings, friends.

Home One—Flood or Drought

Picture this home from your memory. Who lived there?

_____

_____

_____

_____

Who was the favorite? _____

Who showed favoritism? _____

What was done? (Example: Was one child given more attention? Material gifts? The "better" clothes?) _____

_____

_____

_____

_____

_____

Whether you were favorite or experienced drought, how did you feel? _____

_____

_____

_____

Home Two—Overcontrol

Who did the overcontrolling? _____
Give an example of the kind of persuasion that the controller used to get his or her way. (Example: I'm having a heart attack; oh,

my heart is beating so funny. You'll be sorry you didn't do the simple things I ask.) _____

_____

_____

_____

_____

_____

How did your "bondage" to this person affect the other relationships in your life? (Example: with spouse, friend, or children.)

_____

_____

_____

_____

_____

_____

If you ever had the courage to confront this person, what did you do? _____

_____

_____

_____

_____

_____

How successful were you in breaking free? _____

_____

_____

_____

_____

_____

Home Three—Blessing Just Out of Reach

Recall conversations between you and your parents. What words and actions did they use to express their expectations of you? Consider the following areas:

Scholastic achievement _____

_____

_____

_____

Sports activities _____

_____

_____

_____

School government participation _____

_____

_____

_____

Social events _____

_____

_____

_____

An after-school job _____

_____

_____

_____

How did you feel about your parents' expectations? _____

_____

_____

_____

_____

Home Four—Punishing Personality

Did the person in your life punish with silence or with anger and abuse? _____

_____

Give an example of an incident. _____

_____

_____

_____

_____

_____

What effect did it have on you? _____

_____

_____

_____

How does it affect you at present? _____

_____

_____

_____

_____

Home Five—Blessing Exchanged for a Burden

In what ways, if any, did one of your parents insist you "earn" a blessing? _____

_____

_____

_____

_____

How did it make you feel? _____

_____

_____

_____

_____

What is the status of that relationship now? _____

_____

_____

Home Six—Emotional Mine Fields

Picture a typical school day. You're just home from school, approaching the front door.

How do you feel? _____

_____

_____

_____

When you open the door, what scene will you see? _____

_____

_____

_____

_____

Who will be there? _____

_____

_____

How will you be welcomed? _____

_____

_____

_____

_____

How do you feel now about the person who left emotional mine fields? _____

_____

_____

_____

_____

Home Seven—Unyielding Family Traditions

Describe a tradition carried out generation after generation in your family. (Example: The eldest son always enters the same profession.) _____

_____

_____

_____

_____

_____

_____

_____

What, if any, tradition were you expected to uphold? _____

_____

_____

_____

How well were you suited—emotionally, physically, mentally—to carrying out the family tradition? _____

_____

_____

_____

_____

Did you comply or defy tradition and go your own way? _____

_____

_____

What happened? _____

_____

_____

_____

_____

_____

_____

Home Eight—Family Secrets

Open your mental closet door. What skeletons rattle inside? (Example: Grandma has cancer, but we're not telling her.) _____

_____

_____

_____

_____

_____

Who knows the secret? _____

_____

_____

_____

Whom is the secret kept from? _____

_____

_____

_____

Why is the family secret so important? _____

_____

_____

_____

How has keeping the family secret affected your life? _____

_____

_____

_____

_____

Home Nine—Partial Blessings

If you were a child of divorced parents, which parent did you live with? _____

How often and how much did you see the other parent? _____

_____

_____

_____

How often and how much do you see that parent now? _____

_____

_____

_____

How did the parent you lived with talk about his or her former spouse? (Did he or she point out and remind you of the good things, or focus on the bad?) _____

_____

_____

_____

_____

In what ways did missing one parent's blessing affect your life? (Examples: distrust of the opposite sex, responding too freely to attention.) _____

_____

_____

_____

_____

If one of your parents deserted the family, which one?

_____

How old were you when he or she left? _____
If you've discovered why the person left, explain. _____

_____

_____

_____

How has this experience colored your life? (For instance, do you always look for that parent wherever you go? Do you wonder what's wrong with you that made him or her leave?) _____

_____

_____

_____

_____

_____

Have you searched for and found this person? _____
What happened? _____

_____

_____

_____

_____

_____

How do you feel about it? _____

_____

_____

_____

_____

If you were an adopted child, how much of the blessing did you receive from your adoptive parents? _____

_____

_____

_____

_____

How important is finding your natural parents? (Do you think about it a lot and strongly desire to find and know them? Have you actually begun the process of looking for them?) _____

_____

_____

_____

_____

If you've found your birth parents, describe the reunion. _____

_____

_____

_____

_____

To what degree did finding them complete your feeling of being blessed? _____

SUMMARY

The people mentioned in this chapter have discovered, as we will later, that help and hope are available for anyone who grew up in any one of these family situations. With the right attitude and information, anyone can find a path from the ranks of the unblessed to the ranks of the blessed.

In the bleak town drawn below, write inside each house the way blessings are withheld.

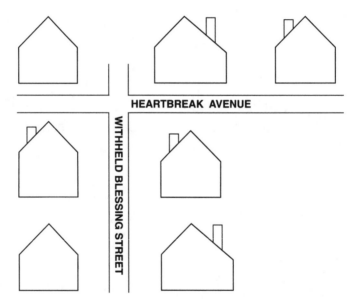

Every one of the elements of the blessing you may have missed can be yours from your heavenly Father.

The journey begins by discovering the reality of a spiritual family blessing that our Lord holds out to everyone and by being willing to courageously face the past.

As you've answered questions in this chapter, you may have dredged up some old angers and hurts. Remember, the intent is to heal, not to blame. Healing will come as you forgive and honor your parents.

Before we consider that aspect of our healing, we'll look at how missing the blessing affects our lives.

Evaluating the Blessing

Getting to Know You

Each person has a natural "bent"—a personality style that determines how he or she acts and reacts. Personality styles or temperaments are generally classified into four separate types—we'll call them lions, beavers, otters, and golden retrievers.

We use the concept of four personality types to learn about ourselves and those we want to bless, but we want to emphasize that behavior can't be neatly categorized to fit into prescribed boxes. No one is exclusively one temperament. We're all made up of a combination of the four types, with stronger tendencies toward one more than others.

A "perfect" personality would be made up of equal parts of all four personality types, as demonstrated by Jesus during His ministry on earth. We'll not reach that during our lives, but we can work toward developing the strengths we have and use them to bless others and to overcome our own missed blessing, if we have missed it.

You can discover your bent by taking the following survey. Put a check mark by the words or phrases in the survey that best describe you. When you are finished, double your score and transfer the total to the boxes below.

Since you may react differently at work than at home, check those phrases that best fit your consistent at-home character traits (at least until you decide you need to give the blessing to those at the office or workplace).

Ellen, whose husband declares she's incapable of making a decision, is a take-charge decision maker where she works. "I don't care what the reactions are at work," Ellen said. "I know what needs to be done, and I push to get it done. At home, I need to know how my husband feels before I make a major decision."

As you do the survey, check those items that actually describe you as you are—with the people you want to bless—not as you wish you were or hope to be.

The Personal Strengths Survey

The Lion

____	Takes charge	____	Bold
____	Determined	____	Purposeful
____	Assertive	____	Decision maker
____	Firm	____	Leader
____	Enterprising	____	Goal-driven
____	Competitive	____	Self-reliant
____	Enjoys challenge	____	Adventurous
____	"Let's do it now!"		

(Total checked × 2 = ____)

The Beaver

____	Deliberate	____	Discerning
____	Controlled	____	Detailed
____	Reserved	____	Analytical
____	Predictable	____	Inquisitive

_____ Practical   _____ Precise
_____ Orderly   _____ Persistent
_____ Factual   _____ Scheduled
_____ "How was it done
in the past?"

(Total checked × 2 = _____)

The Otter

_____ Takes risks   _____ Fun-loving
_____ Visionary   _____ Likes variety
_____ Motivator   _____ Enjoys change
_____ Energetic   _____ Creative
_____ Very verbal   _____ Group-oriented
_____ Promoter   _____ Mixes easily
_____ Avoids details   _____ Optimistic
_____ "Trust me! It'll
work out!"

(Total checked × 2 = _____)

The Golden Retriever

_____ Loyal   _____ Adaptable
_____ Nondemanding   _____ Sympathetic
_____ Even-keeled   _____ Thoughtful
_____ Avoids conflict   _____ Nurturing
_____ Enjoys routine   _____ Patient
_____ Dislikes change   _____ Tolerant
_____ Deep relationships _____ Good listener
_____ "Let's keep things
the way they are."

(Total checked × 2 = _____)

How many check marks did you make for Lion? _____
for Beaver? _____
for Otter? _____
for Golden Retriever? _____

On the chart below, place a dot on the vertical L line that corresponds with the number you checked for Lion; on the B line for Beaver; on the O line for Otter; and on the G line for Golden Retriever. Draw a line from dot to dot.

Personal Strengths Survey Chart

	L	B	O	G
30				
24				
18				
12				
6				
0				

Use this second copy of the survey to have another person—spouse, child, parent, or friend—mark his or her observation of your personal strengths. A second opinion may give you a more objective analysis.

The Personal Strengths Survey

The Lion

_____ Takes charge   _____ Bold
_____ Determined   _____ Purposeful
_____ Assertive   _____ Decision maker
_____ Firm   _____ Leader
_____ Enterprising   _____ Goal-driven
_____ Competitive   _____ Self-reliant

_____ Enjoys challenge   _____ Adventurous
_____ "Let's do it now!"

(Total checked × 2 = _____)

The Beaver

_____ Deliberate	_____ Discerning
_____ Controlled	_____ Detailed
_____ Reserved	_____ Analytical
_____ Predictable	_____ Inquisitive
_____ Practical	_____ Precise
_____ Orderly	_____ Persistent
_____ Factual	_____ Scheduled
_____ "How was it done in the past?"	

(Total checked × 2 = _____)

The Otter

_____ Takes risks	_____ Fun-loving
_____ Visionary	_____ Likes variety
_____ Motivator	_____ Enjoys change
_____ Energetic	_____ Creative
_____ Very verbal	_____ Group-oriented
_____ Promoter	_____ Mixes easily
_____ Avoids details	_____ Optimistic
_____ "Trust me! It'll work out!"	

(Total checked × 2 = _____)

The Golden Retriever

_____ Loyal
_____ Nondemanding
_____ Even-keeled
_____ Avoids conflict
_____ Enjoys routine
_____ Dislikes change
_____ Deep relationships
_____ "Let's keep things
the way they are."

_____ Adaptable
_____ Sympathetic
_____ Thoughtful
_____ Nurturing
_____ Patient
_____ Tolerant
_____ Good listener

(Total checked × 2 = _____)

How many check marks did you make for Lion? _____
for Beaver? _____
for Otter? _____
for Golden Retriever? _____

Personal Strengths Survey Chart

	L	B	O	G
30				
24				
18				
12				
6				
0				

From these two sources, you've discovered whether your character traits more closely resemble the lion, the beaver, the otter, or the golden retriever. You will have, of course, an interesting smattering of the others. You may have rated high in two of the personality types.

On the next chart, complete the survey on your parents or the persons who raised you. There is room for two responses.

The Personal Strengths Survey

The Lion

____ ____ Takes charge	____ ____ Bold
____ ____ Determined	____ ____ Purposeful
____ ____ Assertive	____ ____ Decision maker
____ ____ Firm	____ ____ Leader
____ ____ Enterprising	____ ____ Goal-driven
____ ____ Competitive	____ ____ Self-reliant
____ ____ Enjoys challenge	____ ____ Adventurous
____ ____ "Let's do it now!"	

(Total checked × 2 = ____)

The Beaver

____ ____ Deliberate	____ ____ Discerning
____ ____ Controlled	____ ____ Detailed
____ ____ Reserved	____ ____ Analytical
____ ____ Predictable	____ ____ Inquisitive
____ ____ Practical	____ ____ Precise
____ ____ Orderly	____ ____ Persistent
____ ____ Factual	____ ____ Scheduled
____ ____ "How was it done in the past?"	

(Total checked × 2 = ____)

The Otter

____ ____ Takes risks	____ ____ Fun-loving
____ ____ Visionary	____ ____ Likes variety
____ ____ Motivator	____ ____ Enjoys change
____ ____ Energetic	____ ____ Creative
____ ____ Very verbal	____ ____ Group-oriented
____ ____ Promoter	____ ____ Mixes easily
____ ____ Avoids details	____ ____ Optimistic
____ ____ "Trust me! It'll work out!"	

(Total checked × 2 = ____)

The Golden Retriever

____ ____ Loyal	____ ____ Adaptable
____ ____ Nondemanding	____ ____ Sympathetic
____ ____ Even-keeled	____ ____ Thoughtful
____ ____ Avoids conflict	____ ____ Nurturing
____ ____ Enjoys routine	____ ____ Patient
____ ____ Dislikes change	____ ____ Tolerant
____ ____ Deep relationships	____ ____ Good listener
____ ____ "Let's keep things the way they are."	

(Total checked × 2 = ____)

How many check marks did you make for Lion? _____

for Beaver? _____

for Otter? _____

for Golden Retriever? _____

Use different colored pens to draw the lines on the Survey Chart.

Personal Strengths Survey Chart

	L	B	O	G
30				
24				
18				
12				
6				
0				

The following are strengths and traits of each personality type. They'll help you in identifying more closely which of the personality types you and your parents or guardians possess.

THE LION

_____ Born leader, self-starter

_____ Likes to be in charge, calling the shots

_____ Likes to be challenged, to tackle the "mission impossible"

_____ Wants results immediately

_____ Seldom procrastinates

_____ Makes decisions quickly, sometimes before all the facts are in

_____ Doesn't like to have his or her decisions questioned

_____ Stands up well under pressure

_____ Doesn't mind confrontation

_____ Often intimidates those with less powerful temperaments

Was one of your parents a lion? _____ If so, how did he or she use one of these strengths well to give a blessing? (Example: Because confrontation didn't bother him, he was able to discipline fairly even when it was hard.)

_____

_____

_____

_____

_____

_____

Character strengths, if pushed to an extreme, become weaknesses. In what ways did your lion parent (or guardian) misuse a character trait? (Example: She used her trait of being a born leader in an overbearing, obsessive way, not letting anyone else express an opinion about what should happen. She ruled with an iron hand.)

_____

_____

_____

_____

_____

_____

_____

_____

Which of the character strengths of a lion do you wish your lion parent had used more in giving a blessing? (Example: likes to be challenged, to do a "mission impossible.") _____

_____

_____

Why? (Example: I was impossible, I'd have liked him or her to take me on and help me become a better person.) _____

_____

_____

_____

_____

_____

What else could a lion personality do that would be beneficial in giving the blessing? (Example: Soften up a bit and be more loving.)

_____

_____

_____

_____

_____

_____

THE BEAVER

_____ Reserved, cautious, and controlled

_____ Loves deeply and loyally, but at times finds it difficult to express that love verbally

_____ Likes to do things "by the book"

_____ Wants life to be predictable

_____ Is good at evaluating all sides of an issue before he or she makes a decision and isn't afraid to say no if he or she sees problems

_____ Looks at issues critically, so is a good problem-solver

_____ Has a love of detail

_____ Tends to be perfectionistic and wants things done right— the first time

_____ Tends to slow down under pressure to be sure of not making mistakes; mistakes or the inability to control the environment may make the beaver depressed

_____ Primary time frame is the past—he or she wants everything to happen just as it has always happened.

Was one of your parents or guardians a beaver? _____
What good beaver quality did he or she use to bless you?

_____

How? _____

_____

_____

_____

_____

What beaver quality was pushed to an extreme to become a weakness and so withheld the blessing? _____

_____

Give an example of an incident in your home that shows how this weakness came into play. _____

_____

_____

_____

_____

_____

_____

What do you think is one of most positive beaver qualities to be used in blessing others? _____

_____

How do you see the quality being used? _____

_____

_____

_____

_____

_____

_____

_____

THE OTTER

_____ Fun-loving and outgoing—the cheerleaders of the world, both in school and out

_____ Never does anything in a humdrum manner if there's any possibility of finding a fun way

_____ Motivates others to action

_____ Can be a manipulator

_____ Tends to skip reading the fine print and plunge ahead

_____ Focuses on the future, letting the past be past

_____ Optimistic, always expecting the best

_____ Avoids confrontation

_____ Has difficulty correcting or disciplining

_____ Avoids difficult discussions

_____ Networks well—knows someone in every field who can help out by knowing someone who knows someone else

_____ Needs to be liked

_____ Susceptible to peer pressure or manipulation

If one of your parents was an otter, how did he or she use an otter quality to bless? _____

_____

_____

_____

_____

_____

How did one of his or her otter weaknesses result in your missing the blessing? _____

_____

_____

_____

_____

_____

_____

Choose one otter trait and describe how it could be used to bless others. _____

_____

_____

_____

_____

_____

_____

THE GOLDEN RETRIEVER

_____ Can absorb vast amounts of emotional pain and relational trouble and still remain loyal

_____ Has strong needs for close relationships that go deep and last forever

_____ Wants to please friends and family

_____ Feels deep compassion for anyone who is hurting

_____ Adapts to any situation—sometimes too much so

_____ Doesn't like change and prefers to be warned of coming change

_____ Holds stubbornly to what he or she feels is right; you can lead this type anywhere, but push him or her nowhere

If one of your parents or guardians was a golden retriever, relate an incident to show how one of the personality strengths was used to bless you. _____

_____

_____

_____

_____

_____

Show, by relating an incident, how one of these traits became a weakness that withheld the blessing from you. _____

_____

_____

_____

_____

_____

What do you think would be a special trait by which a golden retriever could bless others? _____

_____

_____

_____

_____

_____

_____

We've included the following chart so you can take the survey on those you wish to bless: children, spouse, or friends. Make as many copies of this chart as you would like for your personal use.

The Personal Strengths Survey

The Lion

____ Takes charge   ____ Bold
____ Determined   ____ Purposeful
____ Assertive   ____ Decision maker
____ Firm   ____ Leader
____ Enterprising   ____ Goal-driven
____ Competitive   ____ Self-reliant
____ Enjoys challenge   ____ Adventurous
____ "Let's do it now!"

(Total checked × 2 = ____)

The Beaver

____ Deliberate   ____ Discerning
____ Controlled   ____ Detailed
____ Reserved   ____ Analytical

_____ Predictable   _____ Inquisitive
_____ Practical   _____ Precise
_____ Orderly   _____ Persistent
_____ Factual   _____ Scheduled
_____ "How was it done
in the past?"

(Total checked × 2 = _____)

The Otter

_____ Takes risks   _____ Fun-loving
_____ Visionary   _____ Likes variety
_____ Motivator   _____ Enjoys change
_____ Energetic   _____ Creative
_____ Very verbal   _____ Group-oriented
_____ Promoter   _____ Mixes easily
_____ Avoids details   _____ Optimistic
_____ "Trust me! It'll
work out!"

(Total checked × 2 = _____)

The Golden Retriever

_____ Loyal   _____ Adaptable
_____ Nondemanding   _____ Sympathetic
_____ Even-keeled   _____ Thoughtful
_____ Avoids conflict   _____ Nurturing
_____ Enjoys routine   _____ Patient
_____ Dislikes change   _____ Tolerant
_____ Deep relationships   _____ Good listener
_____ "Let's keep things
the way they are."

(Total checked × 2 = _____)

How many check marks did you make for Lion? _____

for Beaver? _____

for Otter? _____

for Golden Retriever? _____

Personal Strengths Survey Chart

	L	B	O	G
30				
24				
18				
12				
6				
0				

The advantage of knowing the temperament and strengths of those you wish to bless is that you can learn how to give each one the blessing more effictively. If some of them have already missed the blessing, you can learn how to help them overcome that lack.

Give an example of one way you could effectively bless each of the personalities.

Lion

(Example: Praise him for his ability to make decisions and how comforting it is to have him do so.)

_____

_____

_____

_____

_____

Beaver

_____

_____

_____

_____

Otter

_____

_____

_____

_____

Golden Retriever

_____

_____

_____

_____

We discuss blessing a person according to their personality makeup in-depth in our books _The Two Sides of Love_ (Focus on the Family, 1990) and in _The Treasure Tree_ (Dallas: Word, 1992).

In the next chapter, we'll look at some of the ways the different personality types respond to missing the blessing and how we can help them.

Missing the Blessing

What happens when someone misses the blessing?

The answer depends on individual circumstances, the way the blessing was withheld, how much of the blessing was withheld, and the personality traits of both the parent and the child who missed the blessing.

We have discovered seven common effects of missing the blessing. Any of the personality types can react in any one of the seven ways, but some have a stronger tendency to react one way than the other. Each effect is accompanied by the personality type that most often reacts that way, but that doesn't mean they are the only ones with those problems.

As you read through descriptions of each of these personality types, check the title box of the ones that relate to you, as you did for the homes that withhold blessings. If you or someone you want to bless fit one of these categories, respond to the questions that follow the description.

SEEKERS

Seekers search for intimacy, but are seldom able to tolerate it. These people feel tremendous fulfillment in the thrill of courtship;

but, after marriage, they can't abide comfortably in the close relationship. Lack of acceptance from their parents has made them uncomfortable in receiving love and approval from a spouse. Although, in general, a spouse can fill almost eighty percent of a missed parental blessing, a seeker is unable to accept even that much.

Never sure of how acceptance "feels," they are never satisfied with wearing it too long in a relationship. They even struggle with believing God's unchanging love for them because of the lack of permanence in the blessing in their early lives.

Hal is a good example. In college, he sought the acceptance he had never received from his parents. He was a cheerleader and was involved in student activities, government, and fraternity life. He dated constantly. He sought intimacy. But every time he and a girl got serious, he'd panic and run. He broke three engagements before he finally got married.

Only a few months into his marriage, Hal took a traveling job to escape the intimacy demanded by marriage. His next step led him into the quagmire of pornography, which offers an illusion of intimacy, but without substance. From there it was but a short slide into seeking intimacy with prostitutes.

Hal is a seeker who can't find the intimacy and acceptance he's looking for. He will go on seeking acceptance for the rest of his life unless he can come to an intimate relationship with God.

Anyone who has missed the blessing may become a seeker, but lions and otters are most apt to become lifelong seekers.

If you are a seeker or know someone who is, write down the evidence you see that identifies the seeker reaction. (Example: *I've always dated, but I chose men who were ineligible for marriage so that I'd never be persuaded to get married. I want the intimacy, but I'm afraid of it.*)

_____

_____

_____

_____

_____

What personality types were your (or their) parents?

_____

Give an example of how the blessing was withheld. _____

_____

_____

_____

_____

_____

SHATTERED

Shattered people live with fear, anxiety, depression, and emotional withdrawal. The shattered person's unhappy road can even lead to the terrifying cliffs of suicide, because those who are shattered are convinced they are destined to be nonentities.

Remember Jim, the young man who so wanted his father's approval that he enlisted and was wounded in Vietnam? His father accused him of getting his "million-dollar" wounds running away from the enemy. That morning on the hilltop, his father's disparaging words shattered Jim.

Both beavers, like Jim, and golden retrievers who miss out on the blessing may become shattered.

Do you know someone who shows evidence of being shattered?

_____

What evidence do you see? _____

_____

_____

_____

_____

_____

Describe an incident that is typical of what led to the person's being shattered. _____

_____

_____

_____

_____

_____

SMOTHERERS

Like two-thousand-pound sponges, smotherers, often lion personalities, react to not getting their parents' blessing by absorbing every bit of life and energy from a spouse, a child, a friend, or an entire congregation.

A smotherer is so emotionally empty from the past that he or she smothers other persons with unmet needs and, like a parasite, drains these others of their desire to listen or help.

Unfortunately, when the people trying to make up for years of unmet needs finally tire of carrying the smotherer's entire emotional weight, the message he or she perceives is rejection. Deeply hurt once again, the smotherer never realizes he or she has brought this pain upon himself or herself. Smotherers end up pushing away the blessing other people offer when they desperately need it.

Eva, a strong lion, is a smotherer. She joined a single-parents group in an attempt to get some of her needs met. Every single parent has need of encouragement and support, and Eva was no different—except she couldn't get enough.

She was welcomed into the group and, for a time, was helped. But, like a typical smotherer, Eva, like the two-thousand-pound sponge, wasn't satisfied. She began calling the group leader ten or twelve times a day. She requested rides from everyone in the group, not only to the group session, but wherever she could dream up to go. She lived for a time on the benevolence fund of the church—in fact, she exhausted every resource the church had to aid single parents.

Eventually the group leader called Eva in after one of the single-parent meetings. He sat down with her and tried to explain gently how out of balance her behavior was and how she was actually smothering the rest of the group.

Eva got upset. Instead of facing her problem and dealing with the lack of blessing, she left the group and joined one in another church. Later, the group leader heard that she'd exhausted that group and moved on to yet another.

Do you know a smotherer, someone who clings and won't let go?

_____

How does this person make you feel? _____

_____

_____

_____

How do you think this person feels? _____

_____

_____

_____

ANGRY

People who are angry at each other are chained to whomever their anger is directed. Many adults are still emotionally chained to their parents because they are angry over missing the blessing. They have never forgiven or forgotten. As a result, the rattle and chafing of emotional chains distract them from intimacy in other relationships.

Many people who are otters, beavers, and lions go into life with a chip on their shoulders put there early in life when they did not experience love and acceptance in their homes.

Marsha is a good example of an angry beaver personality. Marsha's two stepdaughters unwittingly did something that made her angry. She wrote to both and told them how angry she was, what poor Christians they were for having done such a thing, and several more raging comments.

Both girls apologized and tried to set matters straight, but Marsha refused to surrender her anger. She held on to it because not forgiving made her feel she had put one over on her husband's daughters.

Whenever the girls visit their father, Marsha disappears into her bedroom until they leave. She refuses to communicate with them in any way. She even weakens her relationship with their father in order to nurse her anger. Much of her ill health can probably also be connected to the rage festering within.

Do you know someone who is letting anger rule and ruin his or her life? _____

What effect does it have on the person he or she is angry with?

_____

_____

_____

_____

What effect does the anger have on the angry person?

_____

_____

_____

_____

_____

DETACHED

An old proverb says, "once burned, twice shy." This motto is used by some golden retrievers and beavers who have missed out on the blessing.

As a youngster, Rodney was a sensitive boy. He loved art and drawing—loved creating things. Then his dad died, and his mother remarried. Rodney's stepdad was harsh and unloving, totally different from his father. Under the regime of his stepfather, Rodney—in self-defense—cut himself off from all feelings. He gave up art, gave up anything creative, and became a CPA, a career that required a clinical, straightforward, factual personality.

When Rodney's wife complained that he never expressed his emotions to her, never said, "I love you" or "I care for you," Rodney agreed to seek counseling. During one session, he said, "I don't think I have ever had any feelings for my wife. I buried feelings a long time ago and don't feel anything. I don't feel love. I don't feel anger. Those all died when my stepfather took over my life." He turned to his wife and added, "I do love you in my own way, but I don't feel."

After losing the blessing from an important person in his life *once*, Rodney, like many beavers and golden retrievers, spent his lifetime protecting himself from ever being so hurt again. Keeping his wife, children, and friends at arm's length, Rodney protected himself, all right—at the price of loneliness and being unable to bless his wife and children.

If you know a detached person like Rodney, write down some observations you've made about his or her life-style.

_____

_____

_____

_____

_____

How did he or she become that way?

_____

_____

_____

_____

_____

DRIVEN

In this category, line up extreme perfectionists, workaholics, notoriously picky housecleaners, and generally demanding lions and otters. They go after the blessing by trying to earn it.

The only problem is that the blessing is a *gift*; you can't buy it. You can find some counterfeit blessings that are for sale—at an incredible price—but they last only as long as the showroom shine on a new car.

Missing their parents' blessing challenges these driven lions or otters to attack a windmill named "accomplishment" in an illusory attempt to gain love and acceptance.

Take Terry, for example. Terry was hired on with a national firm as a first-level manager. She enjoyed the job and the people she worked with. In fact, one of the men was more than special, and before a year went by, they were married.

But Terry wasn't satisfied. She knew that she wouldn't measure up to her Dad's standards if she stayed at first-line management for long, so she began spending longer hours on the job—ten hours a day, then twelve. She won her promotion to second-line management and felt the thrill of victory—for a short time, until the urge to succeed again drove her.

She added Saturday to her work week. Her husband complained, and she promised him more time if she could just make the next level. She devoted more and more energy to the job. The day she raced home to tell her husband she had made it to the regional level, she found divorce papers lying on the kitchen table.

Her goal was reached—at the cost of her marriage.

Do you know someone like Terry, whose need to succeed is more important than family? _____ What is he or she really trying to earn? _____

_____

_____

_____

_____

_____

What has his or her drive cost in terms of family?

_____

_____

_____

_____

_____

_____

SEDUCED

Many golden retrievers, otters, and some beavers who have missed out on their parents' blessing look for that lost love in all the wrong places.

When Ardis was only five or six years old, her mother would come into her room early in the morning to check if Ardis had hung her clothes up properly the night before. If Ardis hadn't buttoned a blouse right or had put the hanger in backwards or a pair of pants weren't hung smoothly, her mother would jerk everything—*every garment*—out of the closet, wake up Ardis, and make her hang everything up right.

Ardis's father did nothing to stop this perfectionist abuse. He watched what happened but would not interfere with the harshness Ardis's mother showed her. This same treatment continued through Ardis's growing up years, and when she reached high school, she sought for love to fill up the vast emptiness inside her. As soon as a boy was kind or showed her any warmth, she practically fell into his arms. She became immoral both in high school and in college—trying to fill her unmet needs for love and acceptance.

Substance abusers also fall into this category. All too often, a drink or a pill is taken initially to try to cover up the hurt from empty relationships in the past or present. Alcoholism or drug abuse or even compulsive gambling can become a counterfeit way to try to gain the deep emotional warmth that is a part of experiencing the elements of the blessing.

Whom do you know that has been seduced into seeking love through illicit means? _____

What happens in his or her life when the substitute fails to provide the real blessing? _____

_____

_____

_____

_____

Which of these reactions have you experienced?

_____ Seeker   _____ Detached
_____ Shattered   _____ Driven
_____ Smotherer   _____ Seduced
_____ Angry

Record a specific incident that illustrates your reaction. _____

_____
_____
_____
_____
_____
_____
_____
_____
_____

How do you feel when you crash up against the wall of lack of blessing? (For example, if you think you're a smotherer, whom do you turn to for release; if you're driven, what kind of activity do you dive into?) _____

_____
_____
_____
_____
_____
_____
_____

How has your reaction to having missed the blessing affected your relationships with members of your family?

_____

_____

_____

_____

_____

_____

Discuss one insight you've gained into your own behavior.

_____

_____

_____

_____

_____

_____

As you've undoubtedly realized, none of these response types—seekers, shattered, smotherers, angry, detached, driven, or seduced people—do anything to resolve the problem. Resolution comes when we turn to our heavenly Father for His blessing and then learn to bless others.

Who needs our blessing? We'll explore that in the next chapter.

7

Giving the Blessing to Others

At the end of a class I (John) was teaching, one woman handed me this note:

> Dennis has learned so much about how to "bless" the children. It has made a real difference in his relationship with them. How about teaching him how to bless me!!!

This woman's request was right on target. The elements of the blessing are not limited to the parent/child relationship. They are essential as the heart of *any* healthy relationship.

WHY DO WE BLESS?

We bless because we follow God's example and the example of God's people. Consider the following passages of Scripture.

"So God created man in his own image, in the image of God he created him; male and female he created them. God blessed them and said to them, "Be fruitful and increase in number" (Gen. 1:27–28).

"So Noah came out, together with his sons and his wife and his sons' wives. Then Noah built an altar to the LORD. . . . Then God blessed Noah and his sons" (Gen. 8:18–9:1).

"I will make you into a great nation and I will bless you;/I will make your name great, and you will be a blessing" (Gen. 12:2).

What is the common element in these three passages?

_____

_____

_____

_____

_____

What insights do you gain into God's feelings toward human beings? _____

_____

_____

_____

_____

_____

When Isaac and Rebekah sent Jacob off to Paddan Aram to find a wife, Isaac blessed Jacob and said, "May God Almighty bless you and make you fruitful and increase your numbers until you become a community of peoples. May he give you and your descendants the blessing given to Abraham, so that you may take possession of the land . . . God gave to Abraham" (Gen. 28:3–4). Put Isaac's blessing of Jacob into your own words. _____

_____

_____

_____

_____

_____

"Now be pleased to bless the house of your servant [David], that it may continue forever in your sight; for you, O Sovereign LORD, have spoken, and with your blessing the house of your servant will be blessed forever" (2 Sam. 7:29). What blessing did David ask for his family? _____

_____

_____

_____

_____

" 'Let the little children come to me, and do not hinder them, for the kingdom of God belongs to such as these.' . . . And he took the children in his arms, put his hands on them and blessed them" (Mark 10:14, 16). How did Jesus bless the children? _____

_____

_____

_____

_____

In many Jewish homes today, the family blessing is still considered important for communicating a sense of identity, meaning, love, and acceptance. In many orthodox homes, a weekly blessing is given by the father to each of his children. Sharing special meals; kissing, hugging, or the laying on of hands; creating a word picture or using Scriptures to praise a child are common elements of blessing children in orthodox homes today.

At many Sabbath services, the rabbi calls the children forward to receive their blessing. Acting on behalf of the parents, the rabbi lays his hand on the head of each child and recites, "May God bless you and make you as Ephraim and Manasseh."

Since God our Father has blessed us so fully—"Praise be to the God and Father of our Lord Jesus Christ, who has blessed us in the heavenly realms with every spiritual blessing in Christ" (Eph. 1:3)— then we in turn ought to bless others.

Can you think of other examples of blessing we might follow?

_____

_____

_____

_____

_____

_____

We also bless to build and restore relationships. Rosa was one of seven children in a single-parent home. Her mother spent all of her energy working to provide food, clothing, and shelter for her family and had little left over except to mete out discipline when necessary. Rosa's mother was never affectionate or warm.

When Rosa read *The Blessing*, her first thought was not of herself and the blessing she never received, but "I'll bet Mom never got the blessing. *I'm going to give it to her.*" She started by asking her mom if she'd received the blessing from her parents. Mom shrugged and waved the thought aside.

Rosa didn't give up. She planned to give her mother all five elements of the blessing and felt it would take two years to get her mother to respond. Every time Rosa saw her mother, she gave her a hug. The first time, her mom stiffened up and pushed back, but Rosa persisted. Each time she talked to her mom on the phone, she told her she loved her and thought she was special.

At the end of eight months, not two years, Rosa's mom responded to Rosa's "I love you" with, "I want you to know I really love you too." It was the first time Rosa had ever heard her mother say those words. The next time they were together, Rosa experienced her mother's first spontaneous hug.

Now Mom doesn't hug only Rosa; she hugs everyone—the whole family. Her life has changed, and her relationships have improved, thanks to Rosa's determination to give her mother the blessing.

Maybe you've been delaying giving the blessing because those who need your blessing are the same ones who hurt you and withheld the blessing from you. Maybe you've said it'll be a freezing day in August before you'd even talk to your dad or your brother or your Aunt Sally because of what they've done to you.

You might be thinking, if you knew my family or my husband or my grown kids, you wouldn't even consider asking me to give them the blessing.

But we are. Why?

Because the stronger personality always initiates the peace.

Is there someone whom you could reasonably expect to bless you who has not blessed, or maybe even cursed, you instead? _____

_____

How do you feel about that person? _____

_____

_____

_____

_____

You have a choice. You can curse this person in a number of ways—with anger, withdrawal, and so on—and become more chained to him or her, or you can bless him or her and experience dramatic freedom. Which path will you choose? _____

_____

_____

_____

_____

_____

WHOM DO WE BLESS?

Our Children

Obviously, from all we've learned, we're called to bless our children. Old Testament fathers did; Jesus did. Parents are the logical and primary source to give their children the blessing that will endow them with the strength and assurance to become healthy, functioning adults.

The blessing of both parents is vital. A child who misses being blessed by parents can fill up only eighty percent of that vacuum from a future spouse, child, or friend. Something always remains lacking.

Blessing our children needn't be a grand production. It can be quite simple:

Recently, my (John's) daughter, Kari, had a dance recital coming up. For several months, she practiced diligently at her weekly dance class and what seemed like *daily* at home.

Finally, when the dance recital was only one week away, Kari came down with chicken pox.

Too sick to dance and too sad to talk about her disappointment without crying, Kari was heartbroken that Saturday. That is, until the doorbell rang for her.

It was a deliveryman with a simple "pick-me-up" bouquet, complete with flowers and balloons, and the message she keeps in her desk drawer still, "Even though you didn't get to dance today, you're still our favorite dancer. We love you very much . . . Mom and Dad."

It took all of three minutes for me to order those flowers, but it made her whole weekend. And in the years to come, it will provide just one more reminder that every day, *even on those days full of disappointment and hurt,* she has Mom and Dad's blessing.

Our Spouse

At the beginning of this chapter, we saw that our spouses need our blessing. If husband and wife become good at giving each other the blessing, then passing the blessing on to their children is that much easier.

When Cindy and I (John) were first married, I had finished my master's degree and was applying to various schools to go on for my doctorate. I felt confident that I would have my choice of schools. But one school in particular topped my list. Finally, a response came from this university. I opened the letter and began reading it to Cindy.

It wasn't until I was three-fourths of the way through the letter that it dawned on me that it was a *rejection* letter, not an acceptance. I faltered to a stop, all too conscious of my new bride hearing this unexpected humiliation. I felt like a failure.

I stuffed the letter into my pocket and said, "Guess I'd better get off to work. I don't want to be late."

When I returned home that night, Cindy had a favorite dinner waiting for me. Beside my plate was a scroll tied with ribbon. I opened the scroll and read Cindy's handwritten message: It's OK that this school rejected you. Even if every school turns you down, it won't make any difference. I'll still love you. God will still use you to help other people. Your life will be blessed.

Cindy hugged me and whispered, "It's OK, you know. I love you."

What is your spouse feeling right now that could be helped or healed by a touch, a word, or a gesture from you that shows unconditional love? _____

_____

_____

_____

Our Parents

Many of our parents, like Rosa's, need our blessing. We cannot completely fill their cup of missed blessing, but we can start the flow and let our heavenly Father fill it up.

Ruth had missed out on the blessing from her parents. Her father died when she was very young, and her mother didn't know how to pass on a blessing she'd never received.

Unfortunately, she also did not receive the blessing from her husband. She spent her life seeking love, but never believing that anyone really loved her.

Her four children decided that they'd plan an eightieth birthday party as a blessing for their mother so she'd know how much she was loved. They planned carefully, even having all her friends (and there were many) mail their cards to the oldest daughter's home to be put into a scrapbook.

The celebration was held in the fellowship hall of Ruth's church, and it was packed. Before the birthday cake was cut, Ruth's children each spoke a word of blessing, then presented their mother with the scrapbook containing all the cards as well as letters of blessing from each of them.

Ruth still struggled with feeling blessed in years after that, but for at least that one day, she knew beyond a doubt that she was loved.

If your parents are still living, how long has it been since you've communicated with them? _____

What would they most like to hear from you? _____

_____

_____

_____

Our Friends

The most well-known Bible story of friend blessing friend is David and Jonathan. Though Jonathan had every reason to hate David, he loved him and chose to bless him. When his father, King Saul, threatened harm to David, Jonathan warned him and said, " 'May the Lord be with you. . . . May the Lord call David's enemies to account.' And Jonathan had David reaffirm his oath out of love for him, because he loved him as he loved himself" (1 Sam. 20:13–17).

Barney had friends like Jonathan—four of them. They worked with him and cared when they saw he was having trouble in his marriage and with life in general.

The four were going to the Promise Keepers Seminar in Colorado Springs, and they decided they'd take Barney with them. Like the men who lowered the paralytic down through the roof to get to Jesus, these four approached Barney and said, "There's a great conference next week that's designed to help men make a go of their marriages and family. We're all going. We're going to take you along."

Barney said, "Thanks, fellas, but I can't. Things are just too tight at home. We can't afford it."

"We're paying the way, and you're riding with us."

Barney hedged. "I'm not sure how Diana would feel about it."

"We've already checked with her. She thinks it's great. You're going."

With a smile, Barney agreed. "I'd love to." He'd been watching these four and liked the way they felt free to give each other a hug when something great happened or when one was feeling low. He liked the way they related to each other. He liked their warmth and candor.

On the way to the conference, the four friends talked to Barney about salvation and his need to have Christ in his life. Just hours *before* the conference began, Barney became a new Christian.

Today, Barney meets regularly with his four friends who didn't think it was enough just to take him to Promise Keepers or lead him to Christ. They're dedicated to helping him grow in his newfound faith and in learning to bless his family.

We all have friends and acquaintances we could affirm and encourage with our blessing. Name someone you could encourage today. _____

What would be helpful to that person? _____

_____

_____

_____

_____

Our Neighbors

Jesus told us to love our neighbors as ourselves. He clearly showed that anyone He brought into our lives needing help, comfort, or material goods is our neighbor.

Neighbors includes friends—but also includes the clerk at the grocery store, the mail deliverer, the old curmudgeon across the street who's always yelling at your children, the people you work with. We can look at each one God brings into our path and ask, "What can I do to give at least one element of the blessing to this person?" It may be no more than a smile. It could be a cheery word. It could be a ride to the doctor's office. It might be telling them of Jesus.

Consider your schedule for the rest of the day. If it takes you out so that you're bound to meet at least one person outside your circle of family and friends, determine that you'll find at least one element of the blessing. What might it be? _____

_____

_____

_____

_____

_____

THE CIRCLE OF BLESSING

How big can this circle become? Is it possible that if we included too many people, our blessing would be spread so thin that we wouldn't really bless anyone?

It could happen. So we set priorities. The diagram below shows how to focus the blessing where we have the greatest responsibility and then to spread the blessing as far as God enables us.

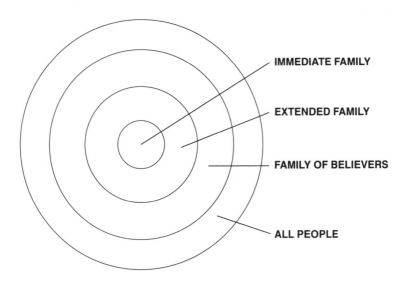

IMMEDIATE FAMILY

EXTENDED FAMILY

FAMILY OF BELIEVERS

ALL PEOPLE

The Inner Circle

Your immediate family is your spouse and children if you're married; if you're unmarried, perhaps it is your siblings or substitute family. They get the bulk of your attention. They need daily doses of all of the elements of the blessing from you.

Singer Mel Tillis has had over twenty #1 hits on the country best-seller charts. His talent and songs have given entertainment to a whole nation, yet Mel said, "My five kids tell me I'm Number One on their list. That's better than any best-seller list, anytime."

We start with those people closest to us, and when we're sure we're number one on their list, then we branch out to others.

The Second Circle

The extended family—parents, siblings, and other family members—is second in priority to hear words of praise and commendation from you.

The first commandment with a promise is, "Honor your father and mother"—which is the first commandment with a promise—"that it may go well with you and that you may enjoy long life on the earth" (Eph. 6:2–3). Honor is synonymous with blessing in Scripture, so we must bless our parents.

Brothers and sisters, perhaps cousins, grandparents, and those related by blood or marriage fall in this category.

The Third Circle

The family of believers is Christians. Many of them will not have received the blessing, and you can bless them using some of the elements of the blessing. Galatians 6:10 says, "Therefore, as we have opportunity, let us do good to all people, especially to those who belong to the family of believers."

As you grow older and your children leave home, you may have time and energy to be a surrogate parent, a blessor to younger Christians in your church. As Paul instructed Titus, we can teach older men to be temperate, older women to teach what is good to younger women, and encourage younger men to be self-controlled (Titus 2:1–6).

The Outer Circle

All people includes those God brings into our lives in divine encounters. These may be few, and you may do much less than you would with the first two circles. You will certainly not give as much time to these people as you do to the inner circle.

In the circles on page 105, write in the names of those you need to bless where they belong.

When do we give the blessing?

At least in this one area, be a lion: do it now!

Sam had grown up in a home that withheld the blessing, so when he had sons, he didn't know how to bless them. One day at a Christian Center he visited, Sam was told about *The Blessing.* He picked

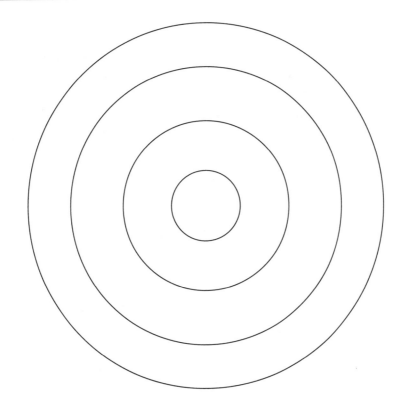

up a copy and realized that this is what he'd missed and he needed to start blessing his children.

Shortly after reading *The Blessing,* he took his fourteen-year-old son, Mike, with him to meet an old buddy who was a stunt pilot. While Mike watched, Sam and his best buddy took off to do some air ballet and stunts. In the middle of a loop, where the plane heads straight up and then falls over backward, the pilot made an error. The pilot didn't have enough altitude to correct his error and the plane crashed to the tarmac.

Mike rushed over and dragged out the pilot, who appeared to be all right. He struggled frantically to get his dad out of the plane and by the time he succeeded, he realized his dad was going to die. Sam knew it too.

Immediately, Sam reached out and took Mike's hand. In the

forty-five minutes before he died, Sam gave all five elements of the blessing to Mike. He touched him, gave him a verbal message expressing high value and a promising future, and spent his last minutes in commitment to blessing his son.

Unfortunately, most of us think we've got forty-five years left, that there's a lot of time for us to give the blessing. So we procrastinate.

Do you procrastinate? Are you putting off blessing your children, your spouse, friends, neighbors, all people?

If you find yourself procrastinating, what is taking so much of your time that you don't have time to bless your family?

_____

_____

_____

_____

How important are these things compared to the well-being of your family and friends? _____

_____

_____

_____

_____

_____

Describe what you feel about giving the blessing. (Example: *I'm a little scared of what the reaction may be.*) _____

_____

_____

_____

_____

What purpose is procrastination serving in your marriage?

_____

_____

_____

_____

With your children? _____

_____

_____

_____

Set a goal to give one or two elements of the blessing to each one in your inner circle. Write down what you will do, with which family member, by when.

Name	Activity	Date

Write down the name of a person you can trust to help you be accountable for carrying out these goals.

_____

Ask him or her to contact you on a regular basis to see if you've done what you plan. Better yet, form a small group of people who are interested in giving the blessing and become accountable to the group.

On the date you specified, check to see if you've carried out your plan. How did you do?

_____

_____

_____

_____

Part Two

FIVE
STEPS TO
THE BLESSING

Step 1—Giving Meaningful Touch

The Importance of Touch

When renowned concert pianist Andor Foldes was sixteen, Emil von Sauer, Liszt's last surviving pupil, came to Budapest and asked Foldes to play. He listened intently as Foldes played Bach's Tocatta in C Major and then asked to hear more. Foldes put all his heart into playing two more pieces.

When he finished, von Sauer rose and kissed him on the forehead. "My son," he said, "when I was your age, I became a student of Liszt. He kissed me on the forehead after my first lesson, saying, 'Take good care of this kiss—it comes from Beethoven, who gave it to me after hearing me play.' I have waited for years to pass on this sacred heritage, but now I feel you deserve it."[1]

Nothing Foldes experienced afterward meant quite as much as the touch of "Beethoven's kiss." It encouraged him to become one of the world's greatest pianists.

If you've experienced a special meaningful touch, record the circumstances. _____

_____

_____

_____

_____

_____

What results did it have in your life? _____

_____

_____

_____

MEANINGFUL TOUCH—WHAT IS IT?

Researchers describe meaningful touch as a gentle touch, stroke, kiss, or hug given by significant people in our lives. Touch becomes meaningful when the one touching desires to bless the one touched and reaches out for his or her benefit, not one's own.

Meaningful touch is appropriate touch. You can hug your own children, but not every child on the block or in the Sunday school. Even if your intent is to bless, the touch must be fitting to your relationship with that person.

In today's society, with abuse, particularly sexual abuse, so rampant, we need to limit touch to what is meaningful, but appropriate. You can tousle every child's hair or give him or her a pat on the shoulder. You can spontaneously hug a friend or clasp hands with an acquaintance. Some people are comfortable with a close hug, while others prefer to maintain space around themselves.

What meaningful touch are you comfortable or uncomfortable receiving? (Example: _I hate being patted on the top of my head, but a hand on my arm is welcome._)

_____

_____

_____

_____

MEANINGFUL TOUCH—WHAT DOES IT SYMBOLIZE?

In the Old Testament, touch graphically represented the transferral of power or blessing from one person to another. For example, during the Day of Atonement, the high priest placed his hands on the head of a goat that was then sent into the wilderness. By this touch, the sins of Israel were transferred to the goat.

When Elijah called Elisha, he threw his cloak over him, conferring blessing and anointing him to become a prophet.

Touch still carries symbolism. What message would you assume from the following scenes:

- A young woman holding hands with a boyfriend
  (Example: *I'm taken. Don't ask me for a date.*)

  _____

  _____

- Two businessmen shaking hands

  _____

  _____

- A father with his hand resting on his son's shoulder in front of a broken window

  _____

  _____

- A father with one arm across his son's shoulder drawing him close and the other holding an umbrella while they wait for the school bus in a downpour

  _____

  _____

- Sisters embracing at the airport with tears on their cheeks

  _____

  _____

- A father walking his young daughter to school, carrying her lunch box. At the school grounds, he hands her the lunch box, stoops with one hand on her shoulder, and gives her a good-bye kiss.

_____

_____

Above all, touch symbolizes acceptance. Read the account of Jesus healing the leper in Mark 1:40–41.

"A man with leprosy came to him and begged him on his knees, 'If you are willing, you can make me clean.'

"Filled with compassion, Jesus reached out his hand and touched the man. 'I am willing,' he said. 'Be clean!'"

The first thing Jesus did was _____
Why do you think this was special? (Note: in Luke's account, he says, "a man came along who was covered with leprosy" [5:12].) _

_____

_____

_____

What was the second thing Jesus did?_____
What does the willingness to shake your hand, to put an arm around your shoulder, or to reach out and draw you close say to you? (Example: _They like me; I'm OK._)

_____

_____

_____

How do you feel if someone refuses to shake hands or touch you?

_____

_____

_____

MEANINGFUL TOUCH—WHAT DOES IT DO FOR US?

Dr. Dolores Krieger, professor of nursing at New York University, has done numerous studies on the effects of touch. What she found is that both the toucher and the one touched receive a physiological benefit.[2]

Repeatedly, Dr. Krieger has found that hemoglobin levels in both peoples' bloodstreams go up during the act of laying on of hands. As hemoglobin levels are invigorated, body tissues receive more oxygen. This increase of oxygen energizes a person and can even aid in the regenerative process if he or she is ill.

Premature infants who are massaged fifteen minutes three times a day gain weight 47 percent faster than those left alone in their incubators.[3] The touched infants cry less, have better temperaments, and so are more appealing to their parents—which is important, because the 7 percent of babies born prematurely figure disproportionately among those who are victims of child abuse.

Touch is stronger than verbal or emotional contact, and it affects almost everything we do. Other studies have shown that meaningful touch can lower blood pressure, protect children from immoral relationships when they grow older, and even add years to our lives.

Stanford University researcher Robert M. Sapolsky has found that meaningful touch during the first three weeks of a rat's life does two things: appreciably increases the length of the rat's life and prevents the usual cell loss in the hippocampus, a region of the brain crucial to learning and memory.[4]

Sapolsky warns that what holds true for rats may not be true for humans, but in the rat population, extra stimulation soon after birth seems to have a lasting effect on the brain, protecting it from damage at the very end of life. Other scientists are finding that warmth and affection during childhood may counter the effects of aging in humans.

Dr. Leonard A Sagan, an Atherton, California, epidemiologist, thinks lengthened life span is due to a rise in hopefulness. "Imagine two babies crying," says Sagan. "The mother of one picks it up, cuddles it, and asks, 'What's wrong?' As a result, that baby feels he has some mastery over his environment. The other baby is left to cry alone in his crib. He feels helpless, worthless, and unloved. And that is what determines whether one will live to be ninety or become an alcoholic and die at fifty."[5]

Beyond physically blessing those around us, meaningful touch determines how we view others and deeply affects our ability to develop good relationships.

How do you feel when someone touches your hand—for example, a clerk returning change?

In one study, librarians were asked to alternately touch and not touch the hands of students as they handed back their library cards. When the students were interviewed, those touched reported far greater positive feelings about both the library and the librarian.[6]

Try your own experiment. When you meet people today, alternately touch and do not touch them. (Of course, you won't refuse a handclasp if offered.) Think about how the touch you offer makes you feel in regard to that person. What did you discover?_____

_____

_____

_____

_____

_____

Even small acts of touch can leave a lasting memory. Which of these examples have you experienced?

_____ Being touched on the shoulder by an adult when he or she walked by
_____ Holding hands with your spouse while you waited in line
_____ Having someone stop and rub your back for a moment
_____ Someone giving you a "high five"

_____ Someone holding your hand in both of theirs

_____ Someone holding both your hands in both of theirs

_____ Someone coming up behind you, covering your eyes with his hands and saying, "Guess who?"

_____ Someone tousling your hair

How did these touches make you feel?_____

_____

_____

_____

_____

_____

WHAT IF WE DON'T GIVE MEANINGFUL TOUCH?

Neglecting to meaningfully touch our children starves them of genuine acceptance—so much so that it can drive them into the arms of someone who is all too willing to touch them.

A common characteristic shared by homosexual men was the absence of meaningful touch by their fathers early in life.[7] Another researcher, Dr. Ross Campbell, said "I have never known of one sexually disoriented person who had a warm, loving, and affectionate father."[8]

Yet another study showed that it takes eight to ten meaningful touches each day to maintain emotional and physical health. In the absence of touching and being touched, people of all ages can sicken and grow touch-starved.

What does this information tell you about the importance of touch?_____

_____

_____

_____

_____

MEANINGFUL TOUCH IN YOUR LIFE

On a scale from 0 to 10, how would you rate the amount of appropriate touching you received as a child? As a juvenile? As a young adult? As an adult? Put a C, J, Y, and A at those spots. (0 on the scale is no touch, and 10 is a totally fulfilling amount of meaningful touch.)

Let's consider the way the amount of touch in your life has affected you.

Write down the circumstances surrounding the first instance of meaningful touch from your parents or another significant person that you can remember.

_____

_____

_____

_____

_____

_____

_____

_____

How did that touch make you feel?_____

_____

_____

_____

_____

Why do you remember it? (Example: *because it was the first time I realized my mom loved me.*) _____

_____

_____

_____

_____

_____

_____

If you felt a lack of touch, record a circumstance where you would have liked to have had meaningful touch and no one provided it. _____

_____

_____

_____

_____

_____

What feelings or inhibitions do you have that you relate to a lack of touch? (Example: *Mom made me feel touch was dirty, so I flinch away from touch.*) _____

_____

_____

_____

_____

_____

The need for meaningful touch does not disappear when we become teenagers and young adults. Often through these years, we may say we don't want to be touched, but deep down, we long for meaningful touch from our parents.

When my (Gary's) son Greg and I were on a talk show together, the interviewer asked Greg for an example of something I had done that Greg really appreciated.

Greg answered, "When I was in junior high, I used to say, 'Dad, I don't want to talk about it, and don't hug me.' Well, I'm glad now that my dad didn't listen to me. What I was really saying was, 'Dad, I do want you to listen to me and I do need you to hug me.' Dad was great. He did the right thing."

How did your parents carry meaningful touch into your teen and young adult years?_____

_____

_____

_____

_____

_____

Did touch become easier or more difficult as a teen and young adult? _____ Why? _____

_____

_____

_____

_____

_____

How comfortable/uncomfortable are you at family gatherings where everyone hugs everyone?_____

_____

_____

_____

_____

_____

How does your comfort level change if you hug or are hugged by someone of the opposite sex versus someone of the same sex?

_____

_____

_____

_____

_____

_____

How comfortable are you with people—not necessarily family—who hug or touch at the slightest provocation?_____

_____

_____

_____

List ways people touch you that let you know they care.

_____

_____

_____

_____

_____

_____

Circle the one type of touch from the above list that is the most meaningful to you. What is meaningful about that type of touch?

_____

_____

_____

_____

_____

In each space write in a benefit of meaningful touch.

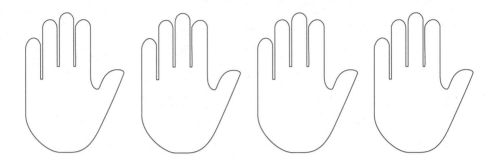

For many people, touching others, even family members, is difficult. If you find it so, analyze why that's true for you. Record your impressions and brainstorm ideas about ways you can overcome the resistance to touch.

Picture yourself in a small group meeting in your church. How comfortable would you feel if you were seated in a small circle so that you were touching three other people knee-to-knee? _____

_____

_____

_____

If you haven't tried this, do so. The effect is most pronounced if you're with people you don't know very well. It has to do with what is called "elbow room comfort zone." Some people need much more space around them to feel comfortable than others.

How much space do you need around you to feel comfortable?

_____

_____

_____

_____

_____

I have difficulty because	Something I can do to overcome that is

How does this relate to your liking or not liking to be touched?

_____

_____

_____

_____

_____

_____

Write a summary statement of how you feel about the touch you have experienced. _____

_____

_____

_____

_____

_____

_____

Complete the following chart to evaluate what kinds of meaningful touch you experience now.

If you have discovered that you lacked meaningful touch as a child, don't give up. You will find that giving meaningful touch fills some of the need of receiving touch. We'll also explore living without the blessing and attaining it through alternate sources in a later chapter.

Meanwhile, in the next chapter, we'll look at ways to give meaningful touch to those we want to bless.

Meaningful Touch

Parents	
Spouse	
Children	
Christian family	
All people	

9

Passing the Touch on to Others

In the last chapter, we looked at how touch or lack of touch affected our lives. We examined information that explained the need for touch and the undesirable results of lack of touch. We analyzed our growing up and adult years to see how much meaningful touch we had received.

In this chapter, we'll examine ways to give this first step of the blessing to our immediate families and others.

PASSING ON THE BLESSING WITH MEANINGFUL TOUCH

Alice almost couldn't stand her preschool son. It wasn't because of anything he'd done, but because he looked so much like his father, who had deserted her before Tommy was born. To Alice, little Tommy represented the biggest mistake of her life.

Alice's rage at Tommy's father all fell on Tommy. When the day-care center where Tommy spent a lot of time was closed, she took care of his physical needs, but she rejected him emotionally. The only time she touched Tommy was in anger.

While studying *The Blessing* in a single parent's class at our church, Alice was confronted with the reality of how she treated her son. She decided to start hugging Tommy.

At home that evening, she held out her arms and said, "Come, Tommy. Mommy wants to hug you."

Tommy ran. His experience was that when Mom reached for him, it was in anger. *So he ran.* Alice didn't give up. She chased him around the house until she finally corralled him and gave him a hug.

Alice persisted in giving Tommy meaningful touch. She stood by the door each morning and insisted on hugging him before he went out to play.

It took over three-and-a-half months for Tommy to recognize that the hugs were there to stay. One day, Alice held out her arms to him from across the room, and he ran into her arms. For the first time, he hugged her and she could hug him back.

Little Tommy was afraid of the outstretched hands because they'd dealt blows, not hugs, in the past. Others shy away from touch because physical closeness makes them uncomfortable.

How comfortable do you think your children are with your touch? _____

_____

Why do they feel this way?_____

_____

_____

_____

_____

What are your children's opinions?_____

_____

_____

_____

_____

_____

What do their actions or reactions show?_____

_____

_____

_____

_____

If your children are growing up in a home where touching isn't done, hugs are nonexistent, and physical closeness is taboo, they will feel distinctly uncomfortable when people get too close even though they will earnestly desire that closeness.

If your children or one child or any member of your inner circle doesn't feel touched enough or doesn't want to be touched, what do you do?

Begin with safe touch. Which of these non-threatening touches have you used?

_____ Touching the elbow, the least threatening or intimidating spot on the body.

_____ A ten-second back rub

_____ Pat a shoulder

_____ Smoothing a hand over his or her hair

_____ High-fives

_____ Grasp a hand, left to right. When you shake hands, right to right, the life flow meets and stops, like magnet repelling magnet. When you touch right hand to left, the flow goes through like an electric current.

What other non-intimidating ways to touch someone meaningfully can you think of? _____

_____

_____

_____

_____

With safe touch, you're making contact, but not so close that you make the other person uneasy.

When your inner circle members feel comfortable with safe, non-threatening touch, take the next step.

List ten different ways you can provide meaningful touch to the people in your inner circle. These should be non-sexual expressions of tenderness, love, and affection.

_____

_____

_____

_____

_____

_____

_____

_____

_____

_____

Don't be discouraged if your efforts meet with resistance. It will take time, as with Alice and Tommy, but the daily effort is well worthwhile.

As children grow into junior high and high school age, they may not want their friends to see them hugging their mom or dad. But as we saw in the example between Gary and Greg, the child will miss the hug if you don't offer it.

I (John) can testify to that also. When my twin brother Jeff and I were young, our mom dropped us off at school every day. When we got out of the car, she insisted on a hug. We thought we hated it. Year by year, my brother and I asked her to drop us off a little farther from school so our friends wouldn't see the daily ritual.

One day, Mom was headed for a major business meeting with a

thousand details on her mind. She forgot to hug us when she dropped us off. Immediately, I, a typical otter, panicked. I was sure she didn't hug us because she'd found out one of many things we'd done that we didn't want her to know about. I worried all day.

At dinner that night, Mom didn't say anything. My brother Jeff, an all-American beaver, wasn't bothered. He could wait forever, but after about five minutes, I couldn't take the suspense, so I blurted out, "Mom, I'm so sorry. Will you forgive me? I don't know how you found out, but . . ."

Mom broke in, "What on earth are you talking about?"

"Well, this morning you didn't hug us. You never made us hug you. I figured you found out."

"I'm sorry, John. I was just up to my earlobes in details for the meeting, but—found out about *what?*"

I was not only in trouble with my mom, but my brother was angry with me too—all over a forgotten hug.

Even if we think we hate it, we don't want to do without that daily touch that says, "You're OK. I love you."

Neither do any of the members of our families.

Turn back to page 105, where you listed the people in your inner circle. Write one name on the first line of each of the sections below. If you need more charts, use separate sheets of paper. If your family is small, just leave some charts blank. Don't get bogged down and discouraged.

Once you've written in the names, answer the other questions for each person, being sure the activity fits that individual.

Name 1 _____

Relationship to you (i.e., son, spouse, parent). _____

Age _____ Where does this person live (your home, his or her own home, same town, across the country)? _____

Describe your current relationship with this person (i.e., close, distant, not speaking). _____

_____

_____

_____

What is your emotional attitude toward this person (i.e., good, estranged)? _____

_____

What is his or her attitude toward you? _____

_____

_____

How do you feel about the relationship (i.e., hopeful, discouraged)? _____

_____

Why? _____

_____

_____

_____

How long has it been since you meaningfully touched this person? _____

Why? _____

_____

_____

_____

In what way could meaningful touch improve the relationship?

_____

_____

_____

_____

_____

What steps will you have to take to make meaningful touch a part of this relationship?_____

_____

_____

_____

How long do you think it may take?_____

_____

How will you start?_____

_____

_____

_____

_____

_____

When will you start?_____

Name 2 _____

What is the person's relationship to you (i.e., son, spouse, parent)?

_____

_____

Age _____ Where does this person live (your home, his or her own home, same town, across the country)? _____

_____

Describe your current relationship with this person (i.e., close, distant, not speaking). _____

_____

_____

What is your emotional attitude toward this person (i.e., good, estranged)? _____

_____

What is his or her attitude toward you? _____

_____

_____

How do you feel about the relationship (i.e., hopeful, discouraged)? _____

_____

Why? _____

_____

_____

_____

How long has it been since you meaningfully touched this person? _____

_____

Why? _____

_____

_____

_____

In what way could meaningful touch improve the relationship?

_____

_____

_____

_____

What steps will you have to take to make meaningful touch a part of this relationship? _____

_____

_____

_____

How long do you think it may take? _____

_____

How will you start? _____

_____

_____

_____

_____

When will you start? _____

_____

_____

Name 3 _____

Relationship to you (i.e., son, spouse, parent). _____

_____

Age _____ Where does this person live (your home, his or her own home, same town, across the country)? _____

_____

Describe your current relationship with this person (i.e., close, distant, not speaking). _____

_____

_____

_____

What is your emotional attitude toward this person (i.e., good, estranged)? _____

_____

What is his or her attitude toward you? _____

_____

_____

How do you feel about the relationship (i.e., hopeful, discouraged)? _____

_____

Why? _____

_____

_____

_____

How long has it been since you meaningfully touched this person? _____

_____

Why? _____

_____

_____

_____

In what way could meaningful touch improve the relationship?

_____

_____

_____

What steps will you have to take to make meaningful touch a part of this relationship? _____

_____

_____

_____

How long do you think it may take? _____

_____

How will you start? _____

_____

_____

_____

When will you start? _____

Name 4 _____

Relationship to you (i.e., son, spouse, parent). _____

_____

Age _____ Where does this person live (your home, his or her own home, same town, across the country)? _____

_____

Describe your current relationship with this person (i.e., close, distant, not speaking). _____

_____

_____

_____

What is your emotional attitude toward this person (i.e., good, estranged)? _____

_____

What is his or her attitude toward you? _____

_____

_____

How do you feel about the relationship (i.e., hopeful, discouraged)? _____

_____

Why? _____

_____

_____

_____

How long has it been since you meaningfully touched this person? _____

Why?_____
_____
_____
_____

In what way could meaningful touch improve the relationship?
_____
_____
_____
_____

What steps will you have to take to make meaningful touch a part of this relationship? _____
_____
_____
_____

How long do you think it may take? _____
_____

How will you start? _____
_____
_____
_____

When will you start? _____

Name 5 _____

Relationship to you (i.e., son, spouse, parent). _____

_____

Age _____ Where does this person live (your home, his or her own home, same town, across the country)? _____

_____

Describe your current relationship with this person (i.e., close, distant, not speaking). _____

_____

_____

_____

What is your emotional attitude toward this person (i.e., good, estranged)? _____

_____

What is his or her attitude toward you? _____

_____

_____

How do you feel about the relationship (i.e., hopeful, discouraged)? _____

_____

Why? _____

_____

_____

_____

How long has it been since you meaningfully touched this person? _____

Why? _____

_____

_____

_____

In what way could meaningful touch improve the relationship?

_____

_____

_____

_____

What steps will you have to take to make meaningful touch a part of this relationship? _____

_____

_____

_____

How long do you think it may take? _____

_____

How will you start? _____

_____

_____

_____

When will you start? _____

Name 6 _____

Relationship to you (i.e., son, spouse, parent). _____

Age _____ Where does this person live (your home, his or her own home, same town, across the country)? _____

Describe your current relationship with this person (i.e., close, distant, not speaking). _____

_____

_____

What is your emotional attitude toward this person (i.e., good, estranged)? _____

_____

What is his or her attitude toward you? _____

_____

_____

How do you feel about the relationship (i.e., hopeful, discouraged)? _____

_____

Why? _____

_____

_____

_____

How long has it been since you meaningfully touched this person? _____

Why?_____

_____

_____

_____

In what way could meaningful touch improve the relationship?

_____

_____

_____

_____

What steps will you have to take to make meaningful touch a part of this relationship? _____

_____

_____

_____

How long do you think it may take? _____

_____

How will you start? _____

_____

_____

_____

_____

_____

When will you start? _____

May God bless you as you seek to put meaningful touch into the lives of your immediate family.

Let's go on to the next step of giving the blessing.

Step 2—Speaking Words of Blessing
The Power of Words

Meaningful touch is more powerful than words, but without the right words, the blessing circuit is never closed and the message of the blessing doesn't get through.

The power of words comes from God. In the beginning, God spoke and all creation came into being. In John 1, we discover that the Word became flesh and dwelled among us.

God has a tremendous desire to communicate with His people. From the time He walked with Adam and Eve in the garden to the commandments to the prophets to the full revelation of Christ, to the Scriptures, God has used words to bless, to inform, to draw, to discipline, to teach.

God always provided a human voice or a written word to let us know His thoughts and feelings toward us. His actions shouted His love to us, but He added His words to make sure we understand. In Jeremiah 31:3, He spoke words of blessing to His people, "I have loved you with an everlasting love; I have drawn you with loving-kindness."

His words are always effective. In Isaiah, we read, "So is my word that goes out from my mouth: It will not return to me empty, but will accomplish what I desire and achieve the purpose for which I sent it" (Isa. 55:11).

Our words also have an effect. They may not always do what we intend, but they're mighty in affecting the lives of those we speak to.

Positive words bless; negative words demolish. Silence can destroy someone who looks to us for a blessing. Both people and relationships suffer in the absence of spoken words of love, encouragement, and support—words of blessing.

Unless a person hears, "I love you. You're special," he or she will never feel completely blessed. Though a parent may shower gifts and material goods on a child and do everything for the best of the child, the child will experience a void that results in incredible heartache and hurt unless the parent's actions are accompanied by accepting, acknowledging words.

Children desperately need to hear a spoken blessing from their parents; husbands and wives need to hear words of love and acceptance on a regular basis from their spouses. Friends need to hear the blessing from friends; parents need to hear it from children.

One word of praise or blessing can last a lifetime. I (John) had a good athletic career during high school, but one coach I had praised me only once in four years.

Twenty-five years later, I still remember the play. I still remember being called to the sidelines. I remember what he was wearing and the hat he had on. He pulled me out for one play to praise me, and it made four years' worth of effort worthwhile many of ways.

THE POWER OF WORDS

How have words affected your life? Do you remember a special event similar to mine? Think back through the years to a time when you felt blessed or cursed. Record that memory in the chart on the following page.

The Power of Words

Event	
Place the words were spoken	
How long you have remembered	
Person who said the words	
Relationship of that person to you	
The words that were said	
Actions that accompanied the words	
How the words affected you—how you felt	

What did your answers tell you about yourself and words of blessing? _____

_____

_____

_____

_____

What can you learn from the exercise about how your words affect the people around you?_____

_____

_____

_____

_____

How might the use of words affect the relationships within your family? (Example: *If we don't use words of blessing, no wonder we're at odds with each other.*) _____

_____

_____

_____

_____

_____

_____

If doing this chart reopened some old wounds, what do you think it will take to heal them?_____

_____

_____

_____

WORDS THAT HARM

If a parent gives a child meaningful touch and says the right words, the child feels blessed. If a parent gives a child meaningful touch but says the wrong words or no words, the child feels a void and will always search for the blessing. The same is true of spouses or friends.

Why? Because words have incredible power to build us up or tear us down emotionally. A parent, spouse, or friend can use the power of the tongue for good. He or she can steer a child away from trouble or provide guidance to a friend who is making an important decision. He or she can minister words of encouragement or lift up words of praise.

But this power can also be misused, sometimes with tragic results. The destructive power of either fiery words or cold silence can affect us for the rest of our lives. Negative words can come from parents who don't care about their children or from parents or spouses who missed the blessing themselves and so don't know how to pass it on. Most of the time, negative words are spoken by loving parents without thought to the consequences.

Demeaning Words

Demeaning words make a person feel less intelligent, less able, less capable, less worthy, less loved, less lovely, less wanted, less of a person. These words destroy.

For each of the demeaning phrases below, picture a scene where they might be said. Then write some words of blessing that would encourage instead of demean. The first one is done as an example.

Clumsy idiot—someone may have tripped or stumbled over something, perhaps banged into something, or knocked a glass full of milk over on the table.

"That's OK, Bobby. Everyone has accidents from time to time. I remember when I was your age. I did [the same thing]."

Dumdum

_____

_____

_____

_____

_____

_____

Why try? You can't do it.

_____

_____

_____

_____

Messed up again, didn't you?

_____

_____

_____

_____

Can't you do anything right?

_____

_____

_____

_____

You're just a bum.

_____

_____

_____

_____

People who hear demeaning words tend to believe them after a time and almost always live down to them.

Harsh Words

Some people hear mostly words spoken in anger—words of abuse. These people are yelled at and sworn at. The Wilson family was like that. Neither Dad nor George, the oldest son, spoke under a roar. Whenever a family member did something to irritate, the whole neighborhood heard about it.

Some families communicate only when they are upset. They develop a volcano-like pattern, like this:

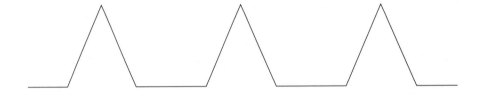

Silence is the norm. When they do have to talk about something serious, there is a big blowup. This is followed by a period of distance and then another blowup.

Harsh words hurt. For all their lives, children may stumble over the hurtful words spoken to them. The words come to memory time and again.

What harsh words do you remember?

_____

_____

_____

_____

Why do you remember them so well?_____

_____

_____

_____

_____

What blessing words would have been more effective in the situation?_____

_____

_____

Some parents who speak harshly insist they're not harsh, only intense.

When I (John) felt strongly about something, my words took on a harsh tone and my forefinger came into play. I pointed at my daughter Keri to stress my point.

When I realized what I was doing, I sat down with my daughter and said, "I don't want my words, even if my motivation is good, to cross the line into harsh ones. If I ever point my finger at you, I want you to know I'll pay you a dollar on the spot."

Keri's eyes lit up. She hoped to be rich in no time. At first, she collected a few dollar bills, but is now dwindled down to three in the past six months.

Empty Words

Some children hear words of blessing, but there is no follow-up. Promises aren't kept, actions don't fit the words, or lack of meaningful touch denies the message. The words lose all meaning, and the child is left unfulfilled. He or she learns distrust.

Which, if any, of these kinds of incidents happened to you?

_____ "Let's go swimming after dinner tonight. It'll be a treat for the whole family." Then, when the dishes are done and you're ready to go, you hear, "No. Not tonight. Dad's tired. We'll do it next week."

_____ "She's [or he's] my little jewel. I don't know what I'd do without [her/him]." But as soon as the company leaves, you hear, "Get out of my sight. What are you hanging around for?"

——— "Of course I love you. You're my child [or wife/husband], aren't you?"

——— "Look, Daddy, see my new haircut!" "Yes, love, it's really neat"—but Dad never looks up from the paper.

What common message does each of these vignettes convey?

_____

_____

_____

_____

Absence of Words

Though the one being silent doesn't necessarily mean to convey these thoughts, his or her silence says, "You're not worth speaking to; you aren't loved."

In a *Parade* magazine article, Burt Reynolds quoted a Southern saying, " 'No man is a man until his father tells him he is.' It means that someday when you're grown up, this man—whom you respect and love and want to love you—puts his arms around you and says, 'you know, you're a man now.' "[1]

Reynolds said of his father, "When he came into a room, all the light and air went out of it. We never hugged, we never kissed, we never said, 'I love you.' " Without the expected words of blessing from his father, he was desperately looking for someone who'd say, "You're grown up, and I approve of you and love you."

Burt Reynolds went on, "I was lost inside. I couldn't connect. I was incomplete. I didn't know then what I needed to know."

Burt Reynolds didn't say why his father couldn't say words of blessing, but most parents genuinely love their children and want the best for them. However, when it comes to speaking words of love and acceptance—words of blessing—they are up against an even more formidable foe than the temptation to speak negative words: overactivity. It can keep parents so busy that the blessing is never spoken. Even with parents who dearly love their children, as one woman we talked to said, "Who has time to stop and tell them?"

In many homes today, both parents are working overtime, and a "family night" makes an appearance about as often as Halley's comet. Life is so hectic that, for many parents, that "just right" time to communicate a spoken blessing never quite comes around.

"Oh, it's not that big a deal," some say. "They know I love them and that they're special without my having to say it." Quite the contrary; to the children, their parents' silence has communicated something far different from love and acceptance.

Some parents feel love, but keep it hidden so deep inside, it doesn't have a chance to surface and pass through their lips. It's as if a giant barrier keeps the words locked inside.

Sometimes words aren't spoken because there are family rules about what you talk about and what you don't—about whom you talk to and whom you don't.

In one family, no conversation was ever allowed to get deep enough to touch real feelings. You didn't talk about things that might make you cry or feel. The unspoken rule was so deeply ingrained that through the years, though Ellen, one of the daughters, could discuss feelings with her husband and others, she felt an insurmountable barrier when it came to conversation with her mother. Now Ellen, in her mid-fifties, is taking care of her mother, who is dying of cancer. The taboo still holds. They don't talk about what hurts most, what is heaviest on their hearts.

Absence of words causes suffering. Unmet needs for security and acceptance act like sulfuric acid and eat away at relationships: between parent and child, between spouses, between friends. The relationships disintegrate.

Perhaps most destructive is the parent who is always home, but never says words of acceptance. This parent sends a double message: "I'm always here, but you can never come to me." By their silence and their actions, such people put a vast emotional distance between themselves and their children. They're in the home, but unavailable.

If you were given the "silent treatment," why do you think your parents withheld words of blessing? _____

_____

_____

_____

_____

How well are you able to express your feelings to others? _____

_____

_____

_____

WORDS OF BLESSING AND YOU

To find out how the words we've been exploring have affected you and how your words affect others, we will look at what kinds of words were or are being spoken. In the following activities, first look at the words your parents spoke to you.

Over the course of your life, which of the following do you feel your parents gave you?

_____ More words of blessing
_____ More demeaning, harsh, empty words
_____ More silence

On the graph below, rank from 0 to 10 how much of each of the types of words you received from your parents. For example, place a dot in the Blessing column for the amount of words of blessing you received. 0 is none; 10 is numerous (which gives you good feeling of being blessed).

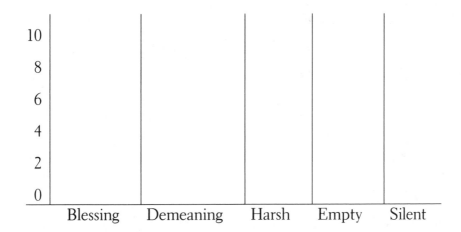

Place dots above each column. Then draw a line from dot to dot. What does this line tell you about the amount of blessing you received or were denied? (Examples: *I received many more words of blessing than I realized,* or *I need to fill up on some blessing.*) ___

_____

_____

_____

_____

_____

_____

How do you think your parents really felt about you?

_____

_____

_____

_____

Are you repeating the same word usage as your parents?

Use this second diagram to show the amount or lack of blessing words you give your spouse (or a friend, if you're unmarried). Have your spouse or friend use a different color of pen or pencil to indicate how much blessing he or she feels he or she is receiving.

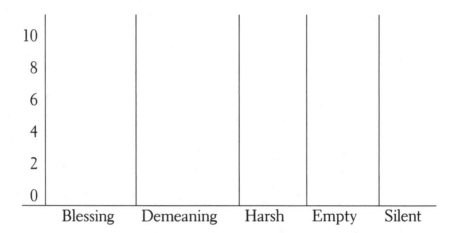

10				
8				
6				
4				
2				
0				
Blessing	Demeaning	Harsh	Empty	Silent

How do these two lines match or differ? _____

_____

_____

_____

_____

What conclusion can you draw? (Example: *My spouse thinks I'm doing a much better job than I think I am.*)

_____

_____

_____

_____

_____

On the next two graphs, explore your perception of your use of words with each of your children (or with other family members if you have no children) and your children's perception of your use of words with them. Use the first graph to chart how you use words. Let your children use the second graph to show how they feel about your use of words.

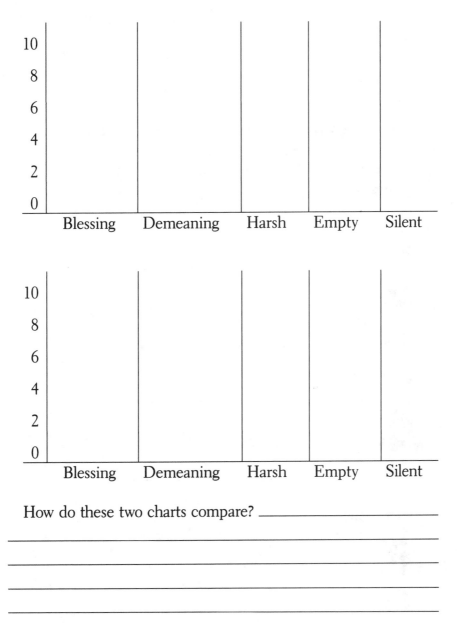

| | Blessing | Demeaning | Harsh | Empty | Silent |

How do these two charts compare? _____

_____

_____

_____

_____

What do you learn from this analysis? (Example: *I'm not doing nearly the job I thought.*) _____

_____

_____

_____

_____

_____

In the next chapter, we'll explore how to improve our scores by giving words of blessing to those we want to bless.

As a review of what we've covered, put words in the mouths of the figures that show:

DEMEANING WORDS

HARSH WORDS

EMPTY WORDS

BLESSING WORDS

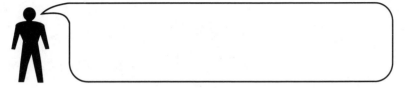

11

Applying Spoken Words

We put spoken words of blessing into practice in our homes and relationships by deciding to speak up rather than clam up. Good words are needed to bestow the blessing on a child, spouse, or friend.

We are not asking you to talk more to your children or others (unless you've been silent). We're emphasizing the quality of what you say: words that bless rather than demean. You need to combine the words with action so they're not empty, but most of all, you need to say the words of blessing.

Everyone of every age—from the delivery room to the mortuary—needs words of blessing. It's up to us to learn to say them to the people closest to us.

For some reason, many of us have to be faced with a trauma before we say the things closest to our hearts. It's possible that with your children, your spouse, your close friends, even with your parents, it's later than you think. In some relationships, it's already late afternoon in your opportunity to talk to someone.

REASONS FOR NOT GIVING A SPOKEN MESSAGE OF BLESSING

So why do we wait? Why do we keep putting it off?

Why do you? Take a little survey.

Write the names of each of the people you decided needed a meaningful touch from you (from Chapter 9). Below each name, write how long it's been since you either said or wrote to that person the words, "I love you," or "I care," "You're special to me," "You're A #1!"

(There are other things we need to say, but we'll learn about them in the next two steps of the blessing. For now, we'll focus on the basic message.)

Next, explain why you haven't given each person a spoken word of blessing. Are you angry with him or her? Are you too busy? Has it been so long, you'd feel embarrassed? What keeps you from speaking words of blessing to each of these people?

Name _____

How long? _____

Reason _____

_____

Name _____

How long? _____

Reason _____

_____

Name _____

How long? _____

Reason _____

_____

Name _____

How long? _____

Reason _____

_____

Name _____

How long? _____

Reason _____

_____

Most procrastination is caused by fear. We might fear the reaction our words will provoke: rejection, amazement, doubt, laughter, or misunderstanding.

If we've never spoken words of blessing, we might get one of the above reactions at first, but if we are as persistent as Alice mentioned in Chapter 9, was with giving little Tommy a hug, it won't be long before our words of blessing are not only accepted, but cherished and expected.

We might fear that we won't seem macho if we say something sentimental. Some parents think they may "inflate their child's ego." Here are other things people fear may happen if they say words of blessing. Mark any that you have felt.

_____ "I'm afraid if I praise them, they'll take advantage of me and won't finish their tasks."

_____ "Communication is too much like work. I work all day, then she expects me to work all night talking to her."

_____ "I just don't know what to say."

_____ "They know I love them without my having to say it."

_____ "If I get started, I'll have to make a habit of it."

_____ "Telling children their good points is like putting on perfume. A little is OK, but put on too much and it stinks."

Most likely the main reason for procrastinating when it comes to giving our children a spoken message of blessing is fear of the unfamiliar. Because our parents never gave the blessing to us, we simply don't know how to do it.

None of these are valid reasons for withholding words of blessing.

How valid were the reasons you recorded for not speaking words of blessing to those in your family? _____

_____

_____

_____

The benefits of blessing our children far outweigh any fears we may have. Don't delay. Please don't let that important person leave your life without hearing the second element of the blessing—spoken words.

Please sign this commitment:

"Today I will speak or write words of blessing to every person whose name I wrote down on pages 161 and 162 of this chapter). Furthermore, I will continue to tell these people I love them and care about them on a regular basis."

_____
Your name

GIVING THE BLESSING THROUGH SPOKEN WORDS

How often do we need to say, "I love you"?

Daily

Like hugs and other meaningful touch, we all need daily doses of hearing words of blessing. At least once a day, we need to lubricate our tongue, clear out our voice box, take courage in hand, and say, "I want you to know I think you're great."

Each night Cindy and I (John) sing a blessing to each of our children. Here are the words of that song:

Good morning, good morning, how are you today?

The Lord bless you and keep you, throughout the day

We love you, we love you, we love you today.

May the Lord bless you, and keep you, in every way.

Keri is now old enough to join in when we sing the blessing to her little sister, Laura.

Another father, Steve, also sings a blessing from the Bible to his year-old son.

Bob blesses his son—not on a regular schedule, but whenever he feels that Christopher is sagging and needs encouragement. When he thinks it's time for affirmation, he hugs tough six-year-old Christopher and says something like, "Thanks for being my son. God loves you and wants you to be the best you can be. Anytime you're hurting, you can come to Daddy and talk."

Often Christopher returns the hug and thanks Dad, but now and then he replies, "I'm OK, Daddy. I don't need to be encouraged today."

How could you give spoken words of blessing? _____

_____

_____

_____

When would be a good time? _____

_____

_____

Celebrations

Spoken blessings can also be given for special occasions, such as a birthday, anniversary, graduation, or wedding. You may want to write the words for these blessings so the recipient can keep them as a remembrance. You want to bolster the ones you bless with pictures of the event and store them in an album or scrapbook.

Over the years, many families have shared their blessing books with us. Three examples stand out.

A thirty-nine-year-old woman inspired her whole family to write letters of blessing to her parents for their fiftieth wedding anniversary. Each member of the family contributed a letter telling his or her gratitude, respect, and love for the couple who'd influenced him or her so greatly.

A sample from their book: "As I add this page to your book of many, I think of how neat it is to have such caring and loving grandparents as yourselves. In the short time we've been together, I've learned so much from you two. . . . I hope that you all know that my love for you guys would fill up this book and a thousand more, and if you didn't know, now you do!!"

Another family member wrote, "Thanking my God upon every remembrance of you—a tribute of love on your fiftieth anniversary from your third-born child. . . . I know I was welcomed into your life. Thanks for making a home for me. . . . I am extremely proud to have you as parents, and I pray God's continued blessing on your lives."

The oldest son in another family, after reading *The Blessing*, involved his brothers and their wives in a project to bless their parents at Christmas. Their blessing presentation included pictures of the families of each of the children, along with words of blessing.

One wrote, "I will always cherish your love and prayerful support. I shall never forget that you used to pray over my pillow. . . . You had been patient with me all through my life, but I knew that you were storming the gates of heaven. I can't help but think that I love to pray because of you."

Each member of this family also chose biblical blessings to add to the presentation. For example, one wrote, "May God grant you, Dad and Mom, your heart's desire. And fulfill all your counsel! We will sing for joy over your victory, and in the name of our God we will set up banners. May the Lord fulfill all your petitions."

The eldest son began the presentation on Christmas morning while one of the others videotaped the scene. The parents cried unashamedly as their son read, "This book was prepared with great love. The time and energies expended in preparation of the sections of this book can never repay you for the love, devotion, and blessings the two of you have given to us. This book expresses a sense of blessing toward you in appreciation of your blessings toward us."

In another Christmas blessing, a young father prepared words of blessing for his wife and each child. He scripted them on pages with decorated borders.

He wrote, in part, "Dearest Palmer, my first born son. I bless you in the name of the Living God and His Son, the Lord Jesus Christ. My heart's desire is that your joy may always be full, that your heart would be overflowing with love, and that your communication with our whole family would be open and rich and full of truth."

Eileen uses the occasion of her own birthday to bless her mother. She sends flowers with a thank-you note for the love and guidance given to her through the years. One year, the following poem accompanied her floral tribute.

> "Thanks for a-bornin' me
> for bearing all the pain
> Thanks for a-lovin' me
> through every stress and strain
> Thanks for a-teachin' me
> all that I should know
> Thanks for a-cheerin' me
> whenever I've been low
> Thanks for a-motherin' me
> through all my growing years
> Thanks for a-keepin' me
> though I caused you many
> tears

Thanks for a-needin' me
 and sharing joys and cares
Thanks for a-holdin' me
 in all your daily prayers."[1]

Whether you choose to celebrate with a large project or just a letter to a grown son or daughter who lives across the country, your written blessings pass on a message of love and acceptance.

Who in your family might need an extra special blessing celebration? _____

Who might help you do it? _____

Suggest one idea of what you might do. _____

_____

_____

_____

_____

BORROWING BLESSING WORDS

If you have trouble coming up with your own words, greeting cards help you say "You're special." One card reads, "I don't think about celebrating you only on your birthday or on the holidays of the year. I hold my thoughts of you within my heart all the time. And do you know what? I think you're wonderful. Today I'm going to tell that to you."

Of course, the words aren't enough. We have to mean them. They must be said with sincerity. They must fit the person we're giving them to.

GIVING WORDS OF BLESSING

Take time to plan a strategy. First to speak or write or sing words of blessing on a daily basis to those loved ones who live in your home. Perhaps you'll choose to write or call once a week to those who live away from your home. And you may want to plan a once-a-year blessing celebration for each member of your "inner circle" of immediate family.

List again the names of those in your inner circle. Then fill in the other information. There may be more forms than you need. Don't feel compelled to fill them up. Don't bog yourself down with too much to do, but figure out a word of blessing for each person in your inner circle.

Name _____

I see (name) _____ every day _____ once a week _____ once a month _____ what interval _____

I think (name) _____ would most like to hear the following from me: _____

_____

_____

_____

_____

This is a sample of words I can say or sing or write to him/her on a regular basis: _____

The best time for me to do this is (bedtime, mealtime, weekly phone call, monthly letter, other)

_____

"I will bless _____ with spoken or written words on a regular basis: daily _____ weekly _____ monthly _____ other _____."

_____

Signature

Name _____

I see (name) _____ every day _____ once a week _____
once a month _____ what interval _____

I think (name) _____ would most like to hear the following from me: _____

_____

_____

_____

This is a sample of words I can say or sing or write to him/her on
a regular basis: _____

The best time for me to do this is (bedtime, mealtime, weekly
phone call, monthly letter, other)

_____

"I will bless _____ with spoken
or written words on a regular basis: daily _____ weekly _____
monthly _____ other _____."

_____

Signature

Name _____

I see (name) _____ every day _____ once a week _____
once a month _____ what interval _____

I think (name) _____ would most like to hear the following from me: _____

_____

_____

_____

This is a sample of words I can say or sing or write to him/her on a regular basis: _____

The best time for me to do this is (bedtime, mealtime, weekly phone call, monthly letter, other)

_____

"I will bless _____ with spoken or written words on a regular basis: daily _____ weekly _____ monthly _____ other _____."

_____

Signature

Name _____

I see (name) _____ every day _____ once a week _____ once a month _____ what interval _____

I think (name) _____ would most like to hear the following from me: _____

_____

_____

_____

_____

This is a sample of words I can say or sing or write to him/her on a regular basis: _____

The best time for me to do this is (bedtime, mealtime, weekly phone call, monthly letter, other)

_____

"I will bless _____ with spoken or written words on a regular basis: daily _____ weekly _____ monthly _____ other _____."

_____
Signature

When you feel comfortable with the basics of saying words of blessing, go on to the next chapter, where we'll look at another element that needs to be part of our spoken blessing.

Step 3—Expressing High Value

The Importance of Expressing High Value

A recent television show told the story of two foster children who were frequently moved from home to home. In one home, they were sent to their room while the family members ate their dinner of roast chicken or steak and potatoes or spaghetti or whatever. When the family finished eating, the foster children were allowed into the dining room to eat their portion of . . . beans.

Without words, the children were shown they were of no value to that family. In their next foster home, they were loved, but so much damage had already been done that the younger child, a boy, had developed aggressive behavior. One day he tried to drown his sister in a backyard wading pool. The social worker was called in, and a decision was made to separate the two. The little girl was adopted, but her brother was shunted off to yet another foster home.

The less value he was shown, the more the boy's anger grew, making couples wary of adopting him. In a vicious cycle, this further rejection dropped his self-esteem to an even lower level.

Like this little boy, if no one else values us, it's almost impossible to value ourselves.

EXPLORING OUR VALUE

Who should have been responsible for blessing you within your family unit? Circle as many people as are appropriate:

father   mother   grandparent   stepparent   sibling   other

If you circled "other," who was it? (You may want to enter more than one name.) _____

_____

The diagram below represents a cutaway view of the rise from sea level to the peak of Mount Everest. Write the names of the people you circled at the place that represents how you felt they valued you. (For example, the foster family of the children in the opening story would rate at sea level—no expressed value, as would a father who deserted you at birth. If your third-grade teacher gave you a great feeling of value, put her name high on the mountainside.)

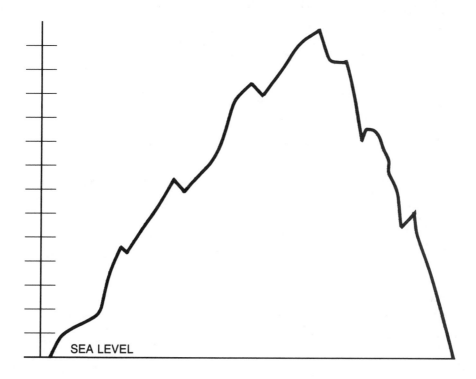

SEA LEVEL

Choose three of the people that have expressed high esteem for you, and complete the chart below.

1. Name _____ Relationship: _____	2. Name _____ Relationship: _____	3. Name _____ Relationship: _____

What words or actions did each person use to let you know you are highly esteemed?

1. _____

_____

_____

2. _____

_____

_____

3. _____

_____

_____

What difference did these words or actions make in your life?

1. _____

_____

_____

2. _____

_____

_____

3. _____

_____

_____

We have all experienced words or actions that let us know we are not highly valued. List three people who did not value you on the chart below.

1. Name _____	2. Name _____	3. Name _____
Relationship:	Relationship:	Relationship:
_____	_____	_____

What words or actions did each person use to let you know you are not highly valued?

1. _____

_____

_____

2. _____

_____

_____

3. _____

_____

_____

What difference did these words or actions make in your life?

1. _____

_____

_____

2. _____

_____

_____

3. _____

_____

_____

Now choose two people: the one who valued you the most and the one who valued you the least. Do you feel your value with these people has changed through the years? _____ Has your value gone up or down? _____ Why?

1. _____

_____

_____

2. _____

_____

_____

How would you describe your *current* feeling of being valued by these two people? (Example: wow!, off the charts, ho-hum, or lower than the *Titanic*.) _____

_____

What are your feelings toward these people?

1. _____

_____

_____

2. _____

_____

_____

What is the status of your relationship with them? (Example: We're really close or I haven't tried to contact them in years.)

1. _____

_____

_____

2. _____

_____

_____

What, if anything, do you think needs to be done about these relationships?

1. _____

_____

_____

2. _____

_____

_____

On a scale of 1 to 10 (1 being no self-esteem and 10 high self-esteem), how would you rate the way you feel about yourself? _____

How well do you like yourself? _____

_____

_____

_____

In general, how well do you think you're liked by others? _____

_____

_____

_____

ATTACHING HIGH VALUE

Every person needs someone to attach high value to him or her in order to feel loved and secure. Solomon, the wealthiest king of Israel, said, "To be esteemed is better than silver or gold" (Prov. 22:1).

Some of the words in the exercise below are synonymous with "to value." Others reflect recognition of achievement or good behavior. Circle the words or phrases that mean valuing a person for who he or she is (i.e., character, attitude, personality):

Rate high	Attach importance
Esteem	Appreciation for doing well
Praise for obedience	Reward for accomplishment
Prize highly	Praise for character quality
Treat with honor	Acceptance

Place a check mark before the words or phrases that recognize accomplishment.

What is the difference between valuing and recognizing accomplishment? _____

_____

_____

_____

Think of a time when you were valued and a time when you were recognized for accomplishment. Which meant the most to you?

_____

Why? _____

_____

_____

_____

_____

What effect did valuing words have versus recognizing words—which made you feel good or made you feel you had to do more to get words of praise? _____

_____

_____

_____

WHAT DO YOU SAY AFTER YOU SAY, "I LOVE YOU?"

We have learned that the blessing must contain meaningful touch and a spoken message that expresses high value. What words express high value?

God, the Father, expressed high esteem for Jesus on two different occasions. When Jesus was baptized, Luke recorded, "The Holy Spirit descended on him in bodily form like a dove. And a voice came from heaven: 'You are my Son, whom I love; with you I am well pleased'" (Luke 3:22).

On the mountain when Peter, James, and John saw Jesus change into a glorified being and talk with Moses and Elijah, God spoke again: "A voice came from the cloud: 'This is my Son, whom I love. Listen to him!'" (Mark 9:7). In recalling the event years later, Peter said, "For he received honor [a synonym for blessing and value] and glory from God the Father when the voice came to him from the Majestic Glory, saying, 'This is my Son, whom I love; with him I am well pleased'" (2 Pet. 1:17).

Which of God's words showed how highly He valued Jesus?

_____

_____

_____

_____

A word, a simple phrase, a pat on the back—it takes little effort, but great awareness, to show people you value them.

Betty shows high valuation of her sister with notes at the end of a letter, such as, "You're special. I'm glad you're my sister."

Other words of value might be, "You're important to me," "You mean so much to me," "You made my day!" or "I'm so excited to hear from you."

What words or actions have you used to make the following people feel highly valued?

Your mom _____

_____

_____

Your dad _____

_____

_____

A grandparent _____

_____

_____

A stepparent _____

_____

_____

A sibling _____

_____

_____

A teacher _____

_____

_____

Your spouse _____

_____

_____

Your children _____

_____

_____

_____

_____

Other _____

_____

_____

_____

Have you used devaluing words with these people? Think back over the past week. What have you said or done that may make one of the above people feel that you don't value them highly? (Example: ignoring one of these people when you knew they wanted some of your time.)

_____

_____

_____

_____

In general, how do the people in your family respond to valuing words and actions? _____

_____

_____

_____

How do they respond to devaluing words and actions? _____

_____

_____

_____

On a scale of 1 to 10, how would you rate the self-esteem of your spouse? _____

Of your children? _____

Of friends (if you don't have a spouse or children)?

_____

How do you influence that self-esteem with what you say and do?

_____

_____

_____

_____

When we realize how strongly words affect us, it becomes increasingly clear how important it is to express high value to those we want to bless—and to everyone God puts in our sphere of influence.

Word pictures offer one good and easy way to do that. We'll learn how in the next chapter.

13

Making Word Pictures

Nancy wanted to bless her husband and tell him how much she valued him. She wanted to be sure he understood just how she felt, so she created a word picture to express her esteem:

> To tell you how much you mean to me, I compare myself to a little girl who made a Christmas list of all the things she wanted most in the world.
>
> On Christmas morning, she woke up and began opening presents. Everything on her list lay around her amidst the crumpled wrappings, but more gifts waited under the tree. She pulled them out and opened wonderful gifts she hadn't thought to ask for.
>
> Ned, my life with you is like waking up to Christmas morning treasures every day.

An excellent way to communicate a message of high value and acceptance—portraying a person's valuable qualities and character traits apart from his or her performance—is using a word picture like Nancy's.

Word pictures are powerful and easy to use, even getting around, over, or through the walls a defensive adult or child can set up. They bring to life thoughts we want to express and multiply the impact of our message because they activate both emotions and intellect.

How many of the following word pictures have you heard?

_____ Sharp as a tack
_____ You have more charm in your little finger than Tilly has in her whole body
_____ One smart cookie
_____ Their elevator doesn't go all the way to the top
_____ Your head is always in the clouds

What word pictures have been used to describe you? (Include nicknames.) _____

_____

_____

_____

Why do you remember them? _____

_____

_____

_____

_____

How did they make you feel? _____

_____

_____

_____

Word pictures can be drawn with one word or with a small story. Both are equally effective at expressing high value. Let's learn how to do it.

MAKING WORD PICTURES

An effective word picture uses a common object—such as a flag, car, or bath towel—or something from nature—an animal, the weather, or mountains—to illustrate the point you want to make. That object, matched with the emotional meaning of the trait to be praised and the interests of the person you are blessing, makes sure the message will get through.

When Jacob blessed his sons, he used word pictures to illustrate how he saw them. Judah was portrayed as a lion, depicting leadership qualities and strength of character. A doe showed the artistic qualities of Naphtali, and Joseph was called a fruitful branch by a spring—a picture of a place of refuge for his family.

You probably already use word pictures unconsciously, but if you don't, you can easily learn.

Take the ever-present smiley face, for example. It could be used to compliment a little girl on her cheerful attitude. Post one on the bulletin board in her room or stick it on the refrigerator door where she can see it and tell her, "You know, Debbie, you're like that smiley-face sticker. Your cheerful spirit brightens my day. Thank you."

- We used an everyday object—a smiley face.
- We valued a character trait—cheerfulness.
- We used the child's interest—something posted on her bulletin board.
- We esteemed the child—you brighten my day.

If Uncle Bill or Grandpa Hanks was a special favorite in the family, you might use him in your word picture. "Son, when you played so hard knowing your team was losing, you reminded me of Grandpa Hanks. He never gave up. He'd be proud of you, and I am, too."

What was the everyday object? _____

What was the character trait? _____

What was the child's interest? _____

How was the child esteemed? _____

Note: If you have more than one child, be sure to make comparisons on equally positive character traits for each one.

Almost any everyday object or nature subject can be a picture to illustrate high esteem. In the chart below, fill in a character trait that could be illustrated by the object.

Nature/Object	Trait
A soaring bird	Imaginative, creative skills
An ever-sharp pencil	
The dining table	
A bedside lamp	
A tulip	

What is good about each trait you've selected?

Soaring bird—(Imagination and creativity soar above the commonplace and lend excitement to everyday life. The person with these traits can unlock doors into the unknown.)

Ever-sharp pencil _____

_____

Dining room table _____

_____

Bedside lamp _____

_____

Tulip _____

_____

Tying these elements to an interest or enthusiasm of the person being blessed catches his or her attention. If you tried to use a bird-watching word picture with a rough, tough football player, for example, you'd fail to affect him.

Choose one of the objects above, along with the character trait you chose, and write a brief word picture that fits one of your favorite Bible characters.

Bible character: _____
Bible character's interest: _____
Word picture: _____

_____

_____

_____

_____

_____

_____

_____

_____

What everyday or nature object might you use to make a word picture to esteem someone for the following traits?

Trait	Object/Nature
Persistence	A beaver—no matter how many times his home is wiped out, he builds again. He always repairs and rebuilds.
Honesty	
Wisdom	
Kindness	
Self-control	

Choose one of the character traits and the object you've selected and write a short word picture about Jesus.

_____

_____

_____

_____

_____

_____

_____

_____

_____

_____

_____

Another way to use word pictures to express high value is to illustrate an undeveloped trait. Jesus did this when he changed Simon's name to Peter ("rock" in Greek). Though Peter wasn't rock-like when Jesus gave him the name, he became a solid, foundational rock after Pentecost.

Assume, for purposes of this exercise, that one of the people in your inner circle possesses the potential for resourcefulness. Think of an everyday or nature item that reflects resourcefulness.

_____

Describe an interest this child may have. _____

_____

_____

Write a brief word picture that shows a person with this interest becoming resourceful. _____

_____

_____

_____

_____

_____

_____

_____

_____

_____

Pointing up the value of a potential strength gives hope. It can be an anchor that the person clings to as he or she goes through trying times.

A WORD OF WARNING

Unfortunately, word pictures of dishonor are just as powerful as those of esteem. Like the foster children who got only beans after the family had eaten steak, those who receive messages of low esteem seldom feel good about themselves.

If the word picture says, "You're no good," the person will feel no good. He or she will lose hope, ambition, and self-esteem and miss out on the blessing.

In the next chapter, we'll learn how to use what we've learned about word pictures to show high esteem to those we want to bless.

14

Learning to Express High Value

Suppose you're not a visually oriented person. If word pictures come a little hard for you, what words would you use to describe your self-esteem today?

_____

_____

_____

_____

_____

_____

_____

_____

Expand on your description by writing a word picture to describe yourself. Here's an example:

Six years ago, I was an acorn clinging to an oak tree. The oak tree released (divorced) me. That fall was the worst thing that had ever happened to me. I crashed to the earth and died in the dirt.

Soon though, my shell broke open and roots of my own began reaching for solid ground. My stem stretched upward toward the "Son." Today, I am a young oak no longer emotionally dependent on people, but on God.

Write a word picture of yourself. _____

_____

_____

_____

_____

_____

_____

_____

_____

_____

_____

How does the way you feel about yourself affect your desire to bless others? (Example: *I've had low self-esteem, but I want to give my family better, so I do what I would have liked others to have done to me.*)

_____

_____

_____

_____

Even if you feel empty yourself, determining to bless others is possible with God's support and brings blessing back to you.

WHOM DO YOU VALUE MOST?

As you recall, you need to attach priority to those you value the most. By placing certain people in that inner circle back in Chapter 6, we put them at higher priority than the extended family in the second circle, the spiritual family in the next circle, and all people in the outer circle.

Underscore or highlight the words in these verses that show some guidelines for who we are responsible to bless:

"Seek first his kingdom and his righteousness" (Matt. 6:33).

"In this same way, husbands ought to love their wives as their own bodies" (Eph. 5:28).

"The wife must respect her husband" (Eph. 5:33).

"Fathers, do not exasperate your children; instead, bring them up in the training and instruction of the Lord" (Eph. 6:4).

" 'Honor your father and mother'—which is the first commandment with a promise—'that it may go well with you and that you may enjoy long life on the earth' " (Eph. 6:2).

List your inner circle people in their priority ranking. Who appears at the top of your list? Where does God *actually* rank? Who comes second, third? Are some people valued equally? If so, put a bracket around their names.

_____

_____

_____

_____

_____

_____

_____

If it would help you, jot a brief note in the right margin to explain why you rated each person as you did. (Example: *Since I have no children, my niece or mother or cousin ranks high.*)

By deliberate decision, we attach value to family, neighbors, and people in our church or our workplace. We must value everyone God puts into our lives and treat them with respect. However, God gives us certain people who need more of our time and energy. For them, we have to plan more specific, in-depth ways to show we value them. Thus, we set the priority rating—who ranks high, who ranks low, who ranks in between—all on a scale of high value.

Attaching high value isn't always easy. The people we need to honor may seem unworthy of our esteem—a mother who deserted us, a child who disobeys and dishonors us, a father who abused us. If judged by performance, these people may not rate higher than a "1.3" on the 1 to 10 scale. Regardless of how these family members treat us, we need to honor them—to respond not by how we feel but according to God's command.

Attaching high value is based on who a person is, not on what he or she does. We must determine to value them just as parents love their children unconditionally, regardless of what they do.

EXPRESSING HIGH VALUE TO OTHERS

Young children learn by repetition. When the Proverb encourages, "train up a child in the way he should go," the Greek word for "train" indicates repeated training. You can tell a child simply and clearly and often. "You're a great son. I love you." "I'm glad God gave you to me to be my very own daughter. He blessed me with you." Singing a nightly blessing, as John does, tells his young daughters he values them.

From your inner circle, list the names of any that are below thirteen. Beneath the name write in word pictures of high value that would make that particular child feel esteemed.

Name _____

High value _____

_____

Name _____

High value _____

_____

Name _____

High value _____

_____

Name _____

High value _____

_____

Practice these word pictures, then use them consistently with your younger family members—perhaps as a bedtime ritual or on waking up in the morning or at a meal.

What about an older child? Simply telling, as you do a young child, no longer gets through. It sounds too much like a lecture. Emotional events and ideas combined with action reach young adults and adults. In other words, this is when word pictures become one of the best means of communicating high value.

This example shows how a mom expressed high value for her son while also showing concern for something the boy had done wrong.

Larry told his mother he was going to a friend's house for the evening. Quite accidentally a couple of days later, his mother, Ruth, discovered that, instead of going to the friend's, Larry went to a party she would have disapproved of.

The next morning, Ruth took her son out to breakfast—something they did frequently. While he ate his pancakes, she said, "Larry, I'd like to ask you a question."

"What, Mom?"

"How would you feel," Ruth asked, "if Betty had told you she couldn't go out with you because she had to do something with her parents and I saw Betty walking into a movie with a good-looking guy I'd never seen before? How would you feel?"

Larry stopped chewing and said, "That would be terrible, Mom. Are you telling me something? Did you see Betty with somebody else?"

"No. This is an imaginary story. I just want to know how you'd feel."

"I'd feel terrible. But Betty wouldn't do that. I trust her. She's the greatest thing since sliced bread."

His mom answered, "Well, Larry, to me, *you're* the greatest thing since "sliced bread." I thought I could trust you, but the other day you did the exact same thing as my imaginary story. A couple of nights ago when you said you were going to Jim's, you went to Ray's party instead."

Larry keenly felt the disappointment his mom expressed with her word picture, and he asked her forgiveness. Ruth both corrected her son and showed him her high esteem with a word picture that entered into his world and interests and used his vocabulary. In a very honoring way, she said something hard softly.

How different and more effective in nurturing her son than what Martha did to her daughter Bekka.

When Bekka came in after family curfew one night, no gentle word pictures waited to build her esteem while being corrected. Bekka arrived home to find every door locked, shutting her out. Not once, but several times, Bekka climbed through a basement window, each time building reserves of anger and resentment against her mother. Neither Martha nor Bekka achieved their purpose: Martha didn't correct Bekka for her misconduct, and Bekka didn't convince her mother she was mature enough to stay out later. Neither gave honor to the other.

If you were Bekka's mother, what word picture might you have drawn to show value while you disciplined Bekka? A little help: Bekka is a senior in high school, wants to be a nurse, and is well above average in intelligence. Martha is a single mom supporting four children.

Your word picture:

_____

_____

_____

_____

_____

_____

_____

_____

Hint: It may be hard for some people to think of a meaningful word picture on the spot. When it comes to discipline along with showing high value, take time like Martha did, to cool down and think the situation through. Then come up with a word picture that communicates what you want to share.

It takes only a little practice to develop skill to use word pictures to attach high value to any member of your family or circle of friends.

Complete this exercise for practice:

1. List your inner-circle people in the blanks below.

2. After you've recorded their names, thoughtfully consider what character trait or quality (i.e., integrity, generosity, trustworthiness) you could focus on to make that person feel highly esteemed. Write in that trait.

3. Write in that person's interests or enthusiasms—something that will give you a direct line to his or her attention.

4. Next, think of an everyday or nature object that demonstrates their good quality. The object is most effective if it relates to the person's special interest or enthusiasm.

5. Write a word picture.

Name _____

Quality/trait _____

Interest/enthusiasm _____

Object _____

Word picture _____

_____

_____

_____

_____

_____

_____

_____

Name _____

Quality/trait _____

Interest/enthusiasm _____

Object _____

Word picture _____

_____

_____

_____

_____

_____

_____

Name _____

Quality/trait _____

Interest/enthusiasm _____

Object _____

Word picture _____

_____

_____

_____

_____

_____

_____

_____

_____

Name _____

Quality/trait _____

Interest/enthusiasm _____

Object _____

Word picture _____

_____

_____

_____

_____

_____

_____

6. When you've made these preparations, rehearse your story. Make sure you have it well in mind, so that it comes out smooth and clear.

7. Pick a convenient time. If your child or spouse is chomping at the bit to dash out of the house to a ballgame or party, you've chosen the wrong time. Give yourself some space to talk. Don't jump in when you're angry or upset.

What would be an ideal time? _____

_____

8. Choose a place without distractions so you won't be interrupted. If the television is on or the person is listening to a loud
radio, you'll never keep his or her attention long enough to get your
word picture across.

Where will you talk to him or her? _____

_____

If possible, sit close to the one you're blessing so you can touch
his or her hand or shoulder. Remember that meaningful touch is a
powerful part of giving the blessing.

9. Tell the person your word picture. Be willing to listen to his or
her response—perhaps a word picture of his or her own to share
feelings.

How did the person react? What happened when you carried
through on this exercise? _____

_____

_____

_____

_____

_____

_____

_____

If you're working with someone hard to reach, someone who has
built self-protecting barriers against all attempts to get inside his or
her feelings, don't give up. Try and try again. Take every opportunity to enlarge on your word pictures to give them more emotional
impact.

Again, a word of caution: word pictures are wonderful to use as motivation to self-esteem. They're also effective at manipulating people to do what you want them to do, but that's an illicit use of this powerful tool. Be careful that your motives are right when you use word pictures to value someone.

15

Step 4—Picturing a Special Future

Self-fulfilling Prophecies

Peter and Patti are siblings now in their mid-twenties. Both are deeply loved by their parents. In most ways, their parents are far above average in giving them the blessing. Both Peter and Patti were given positive-future pictures on short-term activities. Both were encouraged to do their best at whatever they tried.

Patti is one of those relatively rare individuals who knew from childhood what she wanted to be: a doctor. Straight As came easily to her, and she excelled in sports. Her parents are vastly proud of her accomplishments. They encouraged her ambition.

Peter, a year younger, wasn't so lucky. School wasn't terribly important to him, and grades didn't mean a lot. He liked sports but wasn't a star, and he had no driving ambition for a particular career. His great love was skiing.

Near the end of Patti's junior year in high school, she started applying to various colleges. After dinner one night, she excitedly told her aunt and uncle of her plans. Everyone was enthusiastic about her future.

In the midst of the discussion, Peter asked, "What will I do? Where should I go to college?"

His father answered, "Probably nowhere. You'll just be a ski bum." His words were corroborated by his wife's laugh.

The hurt in Peter's eyes was missed by his father and mother. They never dreamed their words caused such deep anguish or such long-lasting effect. In an attempt not to compare and push Peter to excel as Patti did, his parents didn't expect enough of him.

Each child received a mental picture of his and her future. Patti saw a successful career as a doctor. She may have seen herself in a white jacket, stethescope dangling from a pocket, striding down the halls of a hospital answering life-threatening calls. Peter's picture—though encompassing the sport he loved—was of a drifting, hollow, non-producing ski bum.

Today, Patti is fulfilling the future her parents encouraged her to pursue. She's finishing medical school. And Peter? He's a ski bum—just what his father and mother's "hopeless-future" words told him he'd be.

Did you receive more positive word pictures of your future or more negative word pictures? _____

The positive/negative message about the future can be given without words, as in the case of Mike and Doug. Mike had a great deal of musical talent and had made all-state choir. On the afternoon of Mike's performance of the year, his brother Doug had a routine soccer game, not a play-off or a championship game, just a run-of-the-mill game.

The boys' dad, who'd been a pro athlete, chose to go to the soccer game. His decision told Mike, "What you're interested in, what you want to be, and who you are isn't important to me."

As a result of this kind of reaction to his interests and activities, Mike has struggled all his life to feel accepted. He has never felt that what he has accomplished has merit. He's empty of the blessing.

What did your parents' or other significant person's actions tell you about their interest in your future success? (Example: *Mom's willingness to work to be able to afford ice time showed she wanted me to succeed as a world-class skater.)* _____

_____

_____

_____

_____

PICTURING A PRESCRIBED FUTURE

Picturing a positive future has its negative side. A parent forcing a child into an activity or career of the parent's choosing is not picturing a special future for that child. Such a parent is prescribing a set future for the benefit of his or her own needs, not the child's. Our true task is to help our children envision the best possible future they can achieve, not direct them into the career we had or wanted to have.

For example, from the time Jim was able to hold a ball and fit his hand into a glove, his father worked with him to make him a star baseball player. Dad, an ex-major leaguer, was determined that his son would also be a national baseball player. Day after day, month after month, year after year, they worked out together. Jim had the talent. He was good. He made TOPS all-American in high school—the cream of the cream of high school baseball stars.

When he chose a college, Jim went on an academic scholarship, turning down the athletic offers despite his father's anger. He was tired of his dad's making him play and practice on every possible occasion. So he dropped out. He never played one more inning of ball.

The pro-baseball future was his dad's picture of the right future, not Jim's. Though he had the talent to make it in that field, he was so angry at his dad for trying to control his future that he didn't want anything to do with either baseball or his dad. He wanted to make his own way.

If your parents planned your future for you down to the specific college and career, did you follow it? _____

How well suited are you to that career? _____

_____

_____

How successful are you? _____

_____

_____

How much do you enjoy your life? _____

_____

_____

_____

If your parents did not plan a specific future for you, but rather encouraged you to do what your bent led you to, how well are you suited to the career you chose? _____

_____

_____

How successful are you? _____

_____

_____

How much do you enjoy your life? _____

_____

_____

_____

If your parents tried to plan your career for you and you resisted their plan and did your own thing, how well are you suited to the career you chose? _____

_____

_____

How successful are you? _____

_____

_____

How much do you enjoy your life? _____

_____

_____

Which of the three options do you think most blesses a person?

_____

_____

PICTURES IN OUR HEADS

The mental pictures our parents or guardians paint for us—whether negative or positive—stay with us, especially if they're repeated over and over. Normally, we do all in our power to make them come true, as William Glasser's study shows.

In his book *Control Theory*, William Glasser described what he called "a picture album in our heads."[1] As soon as we're born, we begin feeling needs. We don't know exactly what they are, but we know we need something, like whatever it takes to ease that pain in our middle that we'll later learn to call hunger.

We don't know what food is, but we soon discover that if we cry and let someone know we're hungry, we'll get a bottle. We immediately form a mental picture of a bottle and the way it satisfies the craving in our stomach. Next time we're hungry, we'll call up that picture and cry until someone brings a bottle.

As our world expands and we learn more, we experience a wider variety of needs and develop a vast album of pictures of what we think is going to satisfy those needs. Glasser feels that "all our senses combine into an extraordinary camera that can take visual pictures, auditory pictures, gustatory [taste] pictures, tactile [touch] pictures, and so forth. In simple terms, this sensory camera can take a picture of anything we can perceive through any of our senses."

We store in our personal picture albums the pictures of anything that we believe will satisfy one or more of our basic needs. They are explicit pictures, never hazy or general. This personal picture album is the specific motivation for all you attempt to do with your life.

Thus, if someone snaps a picture of a future of promise and success in our mental album, that becomes our motivation to succeed. Likewise, if the future picture is bleak and full of failure, that's the picture that will motivate our actions. According to Glasser, the power of the pictures is total. We may go so far as to choose behaviors that endanger our lives in order to fill our needs from the pictures in our album.

Pictures of the future can be a career or life ambition, or they can be of what's ahead tomorrow and your ability to handle it. When a parent says, "You can do it" about all the small, daily things in life, it builds confidence for the whole future.

Check the statements that most closely fit your upbringing.

The future my parents (or other significant person) pictured for me was

_____ You can do anything you set your mind to.
_____ Of course you can pass the test next week. Let's study together.
_____ If you'd only try, you could make something of yourself.
_____ You're so lazy, you'll never amount to anything.
_____ I know you're scared, but you can do it. I believe in you.

_____ We've always had at least one [doctor, lawyer, preacher, teacher] in our family. I guess you're it.

_____ That's a great goal. Go for it.

_____ Okay, the training wheels are off. I'll be right beside you, but you can ride the bike alone.

_____ It's our family business. Of course, you're going to take over when I retire.

_____ The way you're going, you don't need to worry about a career. They'll keep you in the State Pen.

_____ With your [musical, sports] talent, you could be a [concert pianist, pro athlete] if you put your heart into it.

_____ Honey, that's a great picture. I'll put it on the fridge door so everyone can see it.

_____ That's too hard. Better go for something you know you can handle.

_____ No child of mine is going into such a risky profession. You can be an [electrician, dock worker, teacher, accountant] like your dad.

_____ You're too dumb to have such high aspirations.

_____ You're no good. You'll never amount to anything.

_____ If that's what you really want to do, keep plugging away and you'll succeed.

_____ Don't worry about getting through high school now, just concentrate on doing your best in the third grade.

_____ Other: _____

_____

_____

_____

Though the normal response is to act out the pictures of the future that are predicted for us, some people achieve great success regardless of put-downs by their parents. One such man is Mayer Billy (Duke) Rudman.[2]

Rudman, an oil millionaire, remembers that when he won an oratory contest at age fifteen, his father accused him of cozying up to the judges. "He was always telling me I was no good. My father said I was stupid." Later, when Rudman had achieved success in the oil fields on his own and offered to evaluate his father's oil deals at no charge if his father would visit him every two weeks, his father walked out.

In spite of, or perhaps because of, his father's lack of esteem, Rudman set out to prove himself and his father wrong. He's done it in a big way financially, but after forty years of trying to forgive his father, he hasn't been able to. Though he proved he wasn't stupid, he still feels—at eighty-one—a lack of the blessing.

YOUR SPECIAL FUTURE

How have you done with regard to your parents' pictures of a future for you? Put a check beside the statements that apply.

_____ I fulfilled my parents' positive word pictures.

_____ I fulfilled my parents' negative word pictures.

_____ I made a successful career despite my parents' negative pictures.

_____ I rejected my parents' design for my future.

_____ I failed in my choice.

_____ I succeeded in my choice.

_____ I did not live up to my parents' word pictures.

_____ Other: _____

_____

_____

How do you feel about your parents' influence on what you have become?

_____ I'm angry that their words kept me from reaching my potential.

_____ I'm grateful for their encouragement.
_____ I can't forgive the low value they gave me.
_____ "I guess I showed you" attitude
    _____ Because you succeeded beyond their words.
    _____ Because you failed as they predicted.
_____ Other _____

_____

_____

_____

Changing the pictures in our mental albums isn't easy, but it can be done. The mental pictures we've taken of ways to fill specific needs can be replaced only by something that is reasonably close to the same satisfaction level.

The ability to change the picture of the special future painted by parents depends to a great extent on whether we are lions, beavers, otters, or golden retrievers. It also depends on the intensity with which the parent painted the picture.

If a parent has painted a dismal future picture, it can be changed, as Duke Rudman changed his.

Jim also refused to accept the future pictured by his father, and he's done well. There may be days when he regrets turning his back on baseball and his potential for fame, but he's living his life his way, and he feels good about it.

Hank made no effort to change, but followed his mental picture of a negative future. All his life, from as early as he can remember, his mother planted in his mind the picture of failure. She said over and over and over, "You will never amount to anything."

Now thirty-four years old, Hank says, "I'm bankrupt physically, spiritually, financially, socially, and mentally. How can I reverse these negative word pictures and turn my life around?"

That's Peter's question. It may be your question, too.

Part of the answer comes from God's promise in Jeremiah: " 'For

I know the plans I have for you,' declares the LORD, 'plans to prosper you and not to harm you, plans to give you hope and a future'" (Jer. 29:11). Combined with the promise in Philippians 4:19, "My God will meet all your needs according to his glorious riches in Christ Jesus," God's plan for us gives hope of a special future.

Record an incident when someone, other than your parents, made a positive comment about your future that you appreciated.

_____

_____

_____

_____

_____

_____

Name three of your strengths. (Example: detailed, persistent, resourceful.)

1. _____

_____

2. _____

_____

3. _____

_____

How do you think each of these three strengths could help others in the future? (Example: helpful—I could help someone finish an important project.)

1. _____

_____

_____

2. _____

_____

_____

_____

3. _____

_____

_____

_____

Look up Psalm 103 in the Bible. List all the positive things God says about your future.

_____

_____

_____

_____

_____

_____

_____

_____

_____

_____

_____

_____

_____

_____

Make your own photo album page of a special future. Write in each picture frame below a positive word of a special future.

16

Finding the Right Picture

Today's children are the first generation in history that doesn't believe the future will be better than the past. They can't envision their lives being more desirable or successful than what they see in the present. Menacing clouds hover on the horizon masking their future.

We have a responsibility to give our children or others in our inner circle a picture of hope. Word picturing a special future, backed up with action to fit the words, act as agents of transformation in their lives. Such words help youth change and develop in a positive way.

Don't sell your children or others short. Picture for them the very best they can be—both in the short term and in the long term. Everyone can have a bright future. A physically handicapped child can have great potential, as can a mentally handicapped person. Nurture their dreams. Without pushing beyond capability, encourage each person on your "to bless" list to the maximum of his or her capability.

FINDING THE RIGHT SPECIAL FUTURE TO GIVE

Security in Jesus Christ is the basis for picturing a special future. Be sure those you want to bless have heard the gospel. Pray for them. Take them to church and Sunday school. Teach them to spend time daily in Bible reading and prayer, keeping a journal of what they learn. After this groundwork is laid, you can go further in picturing a special future for each one.

Elaine studied *The Blessing* and determined to bless her husband, Fred; her two sons, Bob and Mark; and her eighty-seven-year-old mother, Agnes.

Meaningful touch and words of love and high esteem had been easy. These were things she'd been doing, but she struggled for a long time over how to give words of special future to her inner circle.

Fred was retired. Bob, a high-school dropout, was now thirty-four and locked by seniority into a job that fell short of his capabilities. Mark, thirty-two, married and a father of one child, had no job. Agnes had lymph cancer and was daily growing weaker and closer to death.

What special future would fit each of these specific people in these situations? After some prayerful thinking, Elaine decided she needed to consider specific information for each one: personality type; how he or she perceived the amount of blessing received; his or her response (i.e., shattered, smothered); interests; and talents. You will want to consider this information when you choose the special future pictures to give those you bless.

You recorded personality types in Chapter 5; responses to missed blessing in Chapter 6; interests/enthusiasms in Chapter 14. To save flipping pages back and forth, copy the information in the space provided here. Then add for each of your inner circle members their talents and any other information that will help determine how to bless each one.

Elaine wrote the following information about her mother. Use it as an example.

Blessing Analysis

EXAMPLE:

Name _____Agnes_____ Personality type _____Beaver_____
Perception of blessing (received/missed) _____Missed_____
Response _____Angry/detached_____ Talents _____Artistic, innovative_____
Interests _____Friends, Bible studies, reading, painting,_____
Other information: _____Afraid of losing independence/too weak to_____
paint or attend Bible studies _____

Name _____ Personality type _____
Perception of blessing (received/missed) _____
Response _____ Talents _____
Interests _____
Other information _____

Name _____ Personality type _____
Perception of blessing (received/missed) _____
Response _____ Talents _____
Interests _____
Other information _____

Name _____ Personality type _____
Perception of blessing (received/missed) _____
Response _____ Talents _____
Interests _____
Other information _____

Name _____ Personality type _____
Perception of blessing (received/missed) _____

Response _____ Talents _____
Interests _____
Other information _____

THE BASICS

Picturing a special future begins with today. The far future will never be bright if we don't give those we bless a sense of confidence and assurance that they have what it takes to accomplish anything they set their hearts on. If, for example, Patti wants to become a doctor, how will she attain the goal if we don't encourage her today in the traits and strengths needed by a doctor, if we don't instill confidence in her ability? We need to work each day to build that special future.

We can do this by affirming each one as a person—giving confidence through acknowledgment of that person's worth—and by encouraging him or her to develop God-given strengths and talents.

Building on the information you recorded in the Blessing Analysis chart (see page 218), write down one thing you can say or do today to start building confidence for the future into each member of your inner circle.

PRACTICE SESSION

If your child had one of the following qualities, what immediate encouragement to develop the quality can you give? What long-term future might you project for him or her?

- A bent for mathematics or science (Example: 1. *You know that math better than I do. I think that's great. You'll pass tomorrow's test with flying colors. 2. You may become an astronaut or a research scientist or a chemist—and maybe change the course of the world.*)

Name	To Say	To Do
Agnes	God loves you and you are His. He does all things well.	Hug often and listen to her concerns

- An appreciation for the ridiculous in life _____

_____

_____

- A loving of reading _____

_____

_____

- Athletic ability _____

_____

_____

• Love of cars and engines _____

_____

_____

_____

• Sensitivity to the feelings of others _____

_____

_____

_____

• Knack for explaining things to others _____

_____

_____

_____

With these ideas for ways to picture a special future and the information from the Blessing Analysis, you're prepared to determine what encouragement and support you can give for the future of the people you want to bless.

Complete the Special Future Chart on page 220. The example given is the special future Elaine decided she could picture for her mother. Her answer can show you how to complete yours.

Picturing a special future is not the same as choosing your children's future. The purpose is to encourage your children to be the best they can be, not—as Jim's father did in grooming him to be a baseball star—to force your children into paths that you followed or wish you had followed.

Parents who put that kind of pressure on children miss giving them the blessing. To give the blessing, encourage your children by supporting their choices and helping them achieve whatever *they* decide to be or do.

BACKING UP OUR WORDS OF A SPECIAL FUTURE

If we have done our homework well and have found exactly the

Special Future Chart

Name	Age	Special Considerations	Special Future
Agnes (mother)	87	Terminally ill, weak	Maintain in own home for as long as possible at greatest comfort level May talk about the wonders of heaven and being with Jesus

right special future words to speak, how well will they be received? How much faith will those we want to bless put into the words they hear?

The answer depends on how well we do what we say we'll do. Check the statements that are similar to things you've done within the past two years.

_____ I promised my son I'd take him fishing, but something urgent always came up and we never went.

_____ I told my daughter I'd look into dance lessons, but never felt it important to follow through.

_____ I intended to babysit with my nephews so my sister could have an afternoon break, but somehow I never got to it.

_____ I said I'd see about getting tickets for the football game, and managed to find some. We had a great time!

_____ I said I'd take my kids and their friends to the zoo. I didn't really want to go that day, but it turned out to be one of the best days we've had together.

_____ I told my daughter I'd make it to her game, but had to make a sales call instead.

_____ I assured both my kids I'd be at the play to see them perform. I forgot all about it.

_____ I told my son I'd help him with the science project. I think I learned more than he did. Wonderful experience.

_____ I said I'd get the kids a puppy for Christmas. They're happy, but my wife's not jumping for joy.

How many "failing to follow through" statements did you mark? _____ How many positive? _____

How much can your children (or others you want to bless) depend on your doing what you say you'll do? _____

_____

Do they count on you? _____ Have they learned to ignore your words because you never or seldom carry through? _____
On a scale of 1 to 10, how would you rate yourself in the past two years with

Child 1 _____ Child 2 _____ Child 3 _____ Child 4 _____

Do you keep your word to each child equally as well? _____

Ask your children their opinion. What numbers do they give you? _____

How close do their answers come to your perception? _____

If the numbers touch the top of the scale, you're doing well, and those you bless can look forward to that special future with confidence.

If your numbers dip toward the bottom, you need to work at keeping your word. You can begin *today* to build the kind of "past" that words of a special future need to rest on by honoring commitments to your children. It may take some time, but with love and perseverance, you can do it.

Although we'll look more deeply at commitment in the next chapters, one specific commitment is vital to assure children of their special futures: your ongoing commitment to your spouse. Over fifty-five percent of children living today will spend some time in a single parent or blended family during their childhood. Words of a special future for a child lose their meaning when a mother or father walks out. The stability of your marriage is directly related to your children's believing you when you say words that picture a special future.

How do your children perceive the stability of your marriage?

_____

When you have disagreements, what actions or words might cause your children to worry about the family being split apart?

_____

_____

_____

_____

Do your children have reason to think that divorce might be considered as a solution to family problems? _____

Why? _____

_____

_____

_____

If yes, how can you change this? _____

_____

_____

_____

If you are already a single parent, what stability do you offer your children? _____

_____

_____

Keeping the family together is perhaps the biggest commitment we can make, but in the next three chapters, we'll look more deeply into the final step of the blessing: an active commitment.

┌─────────┐
│ **17** │
└─────────┘

Step 5—Making an Active Commitment

Offering a Blessing

Like clouds and wind without rain is a man who boasts of gifts he does not give" (Prov. 25:14). We have learned much about giving the blessing. It is time to look at ways to do what we've learned so that we are not unproductive.

If we received the blessing from our parents, it's much easier to give the blessing. We have a good example to follow.

If we didn't receive the blessing, we may do as I (John) do: I bless my children by giving them all that I would have liked to receive from my father and didn't. Others follow their "natural patterning," the inner voice that tells them to parent as their parents did and end up not giving the blessing.

OUR NATURAL PATTERNING

Because so much of our behavioral learning is by example, we develop an inner sense of how things should be done by watching what our parents did.

That's why Alice always puts three cuts in the top of her pie crust or Jane is a rigidly strict disciplinarian or Bob always shaves the right side of his face first or Harry releases his frustrations by yelling at his wife. We do it because Mom or Dad did it. We copy what we grew up with.

Our reaction to any given situation comes from an automatic inner response developed by our past experience. These inner responses are our "natural patterning." If our parenting example did not include giving the blessing, if we grew up in a hurtful or dysfunctional home, we may have been imprinted with a faulty patterning on parenting—or on being a wife or husband or friend.

Our natural patterning affects all we do. If experience taught us the right response to a situation, our inner voice tells us the right thing to do. If what it taught us was wrong, we must use conscious effort to say no to our inner voice and do the right thing, retraining that inner voice.

I (John) grew up in a home where there were lots of positive affirming words. However, hugging or touching was not a consistent part of my family's expression of love and acceptance. When I married and had children, my inner voice said, "Tell them they're doing great; praise them." It never mentioned giving them a hug. Yet, because I knew the importance of meaningful touch, I made an effort to add the hug. Unnatural and uncomfortable at first, hugging became easier as I trained myself to be more affectionate.

As you respond to the following questions, it may be helpful to have one specific person in mind.

How does your natural patterning affect you in the following areas:

Giving meaningful touch _____

_____

_____

_____

Speaking a message of blessing _____

_____

_____

_____

Expressing high value _____

_____

_____

_____

Picturing a special future _____

_____

_____

_____

How do you rate on having a patterning that tells you the right thing to do according to what you've learned in this workbook? (Example: *I'm about in the middle. I score high on meaningful touch, but low on verbal expression.*)

_____

_____

_____

_____

How willing—on a scale of 1 to 10—are you to work at changing that patterning so that you more easily do the right thing? _____
You can commit to work at changing your patterning and, in doing so, begin to offer the blessing to those you love. There are several steps that will help you in making this active commitment to bless others.

COMMIT THOSE BEING BLESSED TO THE LORD

Committing those being blessed to the Lord is the first step of offering the blessing to those we love. Ideally, we commit our children to the Lord before they are born. While our infants are still in the womb, we can say words of blessing to them. Having blessed an unborn child is a big comfort to those who lose a child through miscarriage or deliver a stillborn child.

We can also bless a newborn before we leave the hospital—as Wayne and Peggy did with little Sarah Ann, who had Down's Syndrome.

Many of us did not know the Lord when our children were babies. Or we didn't know about giving the blessing. It is never too late. Our children's blessing can be committed to the Lord at any time, even when they have children and grandchildren of their own.

If you have a newborn in the family—your child, grandchild, niece, or nephew—write words to commit this child to the Lord that you could say as you look at him or her in the hospital nursery.

_____

_____

_____

_____

_____

_____

If your children are older or you are blessing a friend, spouse, or parent, write a blessing you could give him or her.

_____

_____

_____

_____

_____

_____

_____

_____

_____

If you have already committed your children to the Lord, how did you do so? (Example: participated in a dedication service at church.)

_____

_____

_____

_____

_____

_____

What steps will you take to teach your children that God is personally concerned with their lives?

_____ Read Bible stories
_____ Take them to Sunday school
_____ Encourage older children to have a "quiet time"
_____ Teach them the character qualities of God
_____ Pray with them
_____ Pray for them
_____ Be a living example—to the best of your ability
_____ Other _____

_____

Another step in making a commitment to offer the blessing is to commit our lives to the best interests of our loved ones.

COMMIT OUR LIVES TO THEIR BEST INTERESTS

When Lois was six or seven years old, her father worked the night shift as a policeman in a small town. Several of her friends started talking about all the horrible things that could happen to a policeman in the line of duty, the worst being killed.

Lois remembers clinging to her father every night and sobbing, afraid to let him go because she thought he might never come back.

Her father knew how to give the blessing, and every night for over four months, he took the time to sit with Lois and read one story that she asked to hear over and over.

The story was about a fluffy little dog that ran away from home and got lost. At the lowest ebb of life for the dog, Lois would stop her father's reading and sob. Her father, realizing Lois's desperate need for security, responded, "Wait a minute, honey. Wait a minute. Let's read to the end and see what happens to the dog."

Lois let her father calm her tears and read on to the dog's joyous homecoming. Then Lois could slip into bed, comforted and secure in the knowledge of her father's love.

Lois's father was tuned in to her needs and did what was possible to help meet them. He gave his time, energy, and resources to help his daughter through a tough time. The following exercise will help you examine your own level of response to your children's (or spouse's or parents' or another's) well-being.

Answer the following questions with particular loved ones in mind. You might use a different color pen for each person. Fill in the blanks with a number between 1 and 4, indicating your answer to each question. (1 = never; 2 = seldom; 3 = often; 4 = always.)

With your loved ones, do you

_____ Plan your schedule to include time with them

_____ Actively attend or support their hobbies or athletic events

_____ Regularly hug or kiss them

_____ Build their trust by being consistently honest with them

_____ Allow them to borrow your possessions

_____ Smile at them regularly

_____ Seek their forgiveness immediately when you've offended them

_____ Keep their secrets if they want you to

_____ Keep your promises

_____ Act cheerful and encouraging

_____ Make a genuine effort to be on time

_____ Avoid using negative nicknames
_____ Take time to respond to everyday needs and fears

Circle **T** or **F** beside the following questions to gain insight into ways you bless, or withhold blessing from, your spouse.

T or F   I make sarcastic statements about areas of his/her life I think he/she should change.

T or F   I raise my voice when I'm angry with him/her.

T or F   I ask his/her advice for important decisions.

T or F   I lecture him/her.

T or F   I compliment him/her often.

T or F   I correct him/her in front of the kids.

T or F   I seldom praise him/her.

T or F   I tell him/her I love him/her every day.

T or F   I often give up TV to do things with him/her.

T or F   I rarely take an interest in his/her job.

T or F   I often provide quiet time for him/her to "recharge."

T or F   I'm involved in a number of outside activities that don't include him/her.

T or F   I make derogatory jokes about married life around others.

T or F   I often go places and do activities he/she likes and I don't.

T or F   I try to enter into his/her enthusiasms.

T or F   I rarely show any affection for him/her in public.

T or F   I've hit him/her in anger.

T or F   We usually have sex when I want to rather than when he/she wants to.

T or F   I hug and kiss him/her often to show my love.

T or F   I've been known to withhold affection to get even with him/her for a hurt I've suffered.

If you've marked negative statements true or positive statements false, you can see that you are not giving the blessing as well as you could. Perhaps the next exercise will help you change the way you treat your spouse and others you want to bless.

A study from the University of Utah revealed that families who have small specific caring behaviors in their homes are significantly happier than people who don't. If little things couples do in court-ship or when their babies are small get forgotten and neglected as days and months go on, relationships sag and deteriorate.

As a visual expression of your investment in family relationships, carry out the "Caring Behavior" assignment.

Make a copy of the chart for each person you want to bless. Give the blank form to each person and have him or her write in ten small specific things you could do for him or her.

Caring Days Record

Care Giver _____ Care Recipient _____

Caring Behavior   *Date Performed*
(Example: foot rub, do dishes, read story)

_____

_____

_____

_____

_____

_____

_____

_____

_____

_____

_____

Each day, do one of the items. They don't need to be done in any special order.

Your spouse or children may reciprocate and do a caring behavior sheet for you. When the first sheets are completed, set up another set for the next ten days. With this exercise, you'll be filling the love reservoir of each person and building his or her self-esteem.

Discipline

Along with giving your time and energy and practicing caring behaviors, discipline is a critical element in blessing your children.

Wade and Susan agreed on most things in their marriage until it came to disciplining the children. Wade tended to be easygoing; Susan, strict. The children soon learned to appeal to their father to escape the more stringent discipline of their mother.

Jim and Elsie had a different problem. Elsie was afraid her son and daughter wouldn't love her if she disciplined them, so she waited until Jim got home from work, recited all the misdemeanors, and walked away while Jim administered discipline fitting the errors. It wasn't too long before the children dreaded their father's return.

Bob and Cindy had yet another problem. The children were Bob's, and Cindy, as stepmother, was unsure of how much discipline she could give. Bob said he wanted her to instruct and correct the children; but, in practice, he resented what she did. Soon Cindy decided to discipline only according to what Bob stated, such as: If one of the boys didn't do his chores, he couldn't watch TV. Even that didn't work, because Bob felt more lenient when the discipline was needed. The boys resented Cindy's attempts to enforce the rules and gloated when Dad changed the rules again.

One thing is clear: there needs to be unity in discipline. Both parents have to agree and carry out discipline as one entity.

What are your discipline problems and strengths?

Circle **T** or **F** beside the following statements.

T or F   I leave most of the discipline of the children to my spouse.

T or F   I'm afraid my children won't love me if I discipline them.

T or F   I often walk away from a confrontation with my children and feel, deep inside, that they've won again.

T or F   I feel my spouse is being too hard when he or she disciplines the children, even when I know the discipline is appropriate and justified.

T or F   I feel my spouse is too easy on the children and doesn't discipline when it needs to be done.

T or F   I feel I am consistent in discipline.

T or F   I feel my spouse is consistent in discipline.

T or F   I think the means of discipline is different for each child.

T or F   I usually wait until my anger cools before administering discipline to my children.

T or F   My discipline is usually effective in correcting my children.

If you marked the first five statements true, then you may want to look hard at your and your spouse's commitment to bless through discipline. Write out suggestions to help you take a firm but loving attitude toward discipline.

_____

_____

_____

_____

_____

_____

_____

_____

If you answered true to the last four statements, you are on the right track in seeing that your children are blessed through discipline.

BECOMING A STUDENT OF THOSE WE WISH TO BLESS

Persisting in Communication

Too often, we give up too soon. Particularly if we have struggled in our relationships with our children or we haven't been close to them in the past, we must be lovingly persistent in encouraging them to talk.

Think of three things you could do to open communication with those you want to bless. (Example: take them to breakfast—just the two of you.)

1. _____

_____

_____

2. _____

_____

_____

3. _____

_____

_____

Answer the following questions with particular loved ones in mind. Fill in the blank with a number between 1 and 4, indicating your answer to each question. (1 = never; 2 = seldom; 3 = often; 4 = always.)

With your loved ones, which of the following do you do?

_____ Give them the freedom to ask you questions without re-
acting or becoming defensive
_____ Freely express your own inner feelings and thoughts
_____ Say "I love you" regularly and without conditions
_____ Share your personal problems and victories
_____ Laugh together regularly
_____ Watch your tone of voice

Sharing Activities

Sharing activities with our children or others we want to bless
gives us an opportunity to know them better. We find out what they
like and dislike, what interests them, what motivates them, what
turns them off.

On our scale of 1 to 4 (1 = never; 2 = seldom; 3 = often; 4 =
always), mark your score as to whether you do these things with
those you want to bless.

_____ Attend church together regularly
_____ Show an honest interest in their friends
_____ Practice a sport, hobby, or talent with them
_____ Show up at parent/teacher meetings
_____ Volunteer at your children's schools
_____ Sponsor a club activity such as Scouts
_____ Teach them how to bake cookies
_____ Read together

Think of one thing each of those you want to bless would like to
do with you. (Use a line for each person you are blessing.)

1. _____

_____

2. _____

_____

3. _____

_____

4. _____

_____

Ask each one what one thing he or she would like to do with you in the next week.

1. _____

_____

2. _____

_____

3. _____

_____

4. _____

_____

Which of these activities will you work into your schedule this week? _____

_____

_____

_____

_____

The need to keep your word is extremely important. It is worse to schedule an activity and not do it than not to schedule it at all. Don't let this discourage you from planning activities, but let it be a reminder to schedule only what you know you have time to do.

Taking the Initiative in Asking Questions

We ask questions to get to know those we bless well. We may think we know what they're thinking and dreaming; we may think we know their interests and enthusiasms. But keeping up with the changes requires constant attention.

To see how well you know your family or loved ones, answer the following questions for each person with a yes or no. If you answer yes, write in your idea. Do you know what each person:

1. Daydreams about most often

_____

_____

_____

_____

_____

2. Would like to be doing when he or she is twenty to thirty years old

_____

_____

_____

_____

_____

3. Thinks God would like him or her to do for humanity

_____

_____

_____

_____

_____

4. Finds attractive in a boyfriend or girlfriend

_____

_____

_____

_____

_____

5. Likes most and least about school

_____

_____

_____

_____

_____

6. Would answer if asked, "What Bible character would you like to be like and why"

_____

_____

_____

_____

_____

If you answered no to any questions, you need to begin asking questions to discover who your child(ren), spouse, parent, or friend is. If you answered yes, check with the person to see how accurate you are.

_____

_____

_____

_____

You may need to make opportunities to ask more questions.

This exercise will help you determine how well you know your spouse:

1. My wife's/husband's favorite men's/women's cologne is

_____

2. His/her favorite food(s) is (are) _____

_____

_____

3. His/her favorite music is _____

_____

4. His/her idea of the perfect romantic night out is _____

_____

_____

_____

5. His/her idea of a perfect vacation is _____

_____

_____

_____

6. His/her favorite subject in school _____

7. His/her least favorite subject _____

8. What did he/she want to be growing up? _____

9. His/her biggest frustration with the kids is _____

_____

_____

_____

10. The household job he/she absolutely cannot stand is

_____

_____

11. The qualities my husband/wife most appreciates in me are

_____

_____

Have your husband/wife complete the answers and compare them with your answers. If your answers are dissimilar, you may not know your spouse as well as you thought. Record what you think you can do. _____

_____

_____

_____

_____

_____

LISTENING WITH FULL ATTENTION

Put down your newspaper, turn off the TV, lay aside the book, set aside your handwork, and give all your attention to what those you want to bless have to say. Anything less tells them they are of less importance to you.

Using the same scale (1 = never; 2 = seldom; 3 = often; 4 = always) do you:

_____ Seek to hear their real inner feelings without ridiculing them
_____ "Light up" when they come into the room
_____ Seek and value their opinions on family issues
_____ Actively listen to them

Our purpose in listening with full attention is not just to make people feel good. We listen actively in order to be able to take what they share and weave it into words and stories that teach new truths and communicate not only the blessing, but also principles for godly living. We listen in order to understand them and so do those things that will bless.

Our children, spouses, parents, and friends are incredibly complicated people. If we would begin today to list all their wishes, opinions, goals, and dreams, it would take us a lifetime to complete the task. That is just the right amount of time needed to finish the course entitled, "Becoming a Student of Your Loved Ones," a class men and women will enroll in if they are serious about bestowing an appropriate blessing on each person in their lives.

All it takes is a decision to actively commit ourselves to others.

BE ACCOUNTABLE TO SOMEONE WHO WILL HELP YOU CONTINUE BLESSING OTHERS

There's one last key to an active commitment to bless our loved ones: making ourselves accountable to someone who will help us continue what we begin.

Genuine commitment to provide the blessing for our loved ones grows best in small groups. If you can meet regularly with two or three other parents, siblings, or friends who will ask how you did in terms of providing meaningful touch for your spouse or children or parents that week; what encouraging words you spoke that attached high value; or even asking on a 1 to 10 scale how high your commitment was to bless your family this week, you're well on the road to a continued commitment.

With this same group, you can admit your struggles and learn from other people's insights and mistakes. All it takes is the courage to ask honest questions and a loving spirit to share God's truth and your own personal insights.

If you can't find a small group, ask your spouse or a close friend how well you are doing in being a source of blessing to them. You can even ask your children if they're old enough.

The input others give us is a tremendous way to evaluate where we are at the present and give us an incentive to work on areas where we are struggling. Left on our own, most of us tend to forget or sidestep these areas. Faithful friends can help us face things and grow as a result.

Who would you choose to meet with you to work together to better bless your children, spouse, parents, and friends?

_____

_____

_____

When will you give them a call and see if you can set up such a group? _____

The following evaluation sheet can be copied and used with your children, spouse, or in a group to help you get started in the accountability process. Do a check every month or so to see how well you're doing.

Personal Evaluation Sheet

On a scale of 1 to 10, how well are you doing in bestowing the blessing on your loved ones? Circle your response.

1. Do I give them meaningful touch daily?

1	2	3	4	5	6	7	8	9	10
rarely									frequently

2. Do I verbally speak words of blessing?

1	2	3	4	5	6	7	8	9	10
seldom									often

3. Am I attaching high value to the people I'm blessing?

1	2	3	4	5	6	7	8	9	10
low value									high value

4. Have I pictured a special future for their life?

1	2	3	4	5	6	7	8	9	10
seldom									often

5. Overall, my commitment level to fulfill my words of blessing is

1	2	3	4	5	6	7	8	9	10
very low									very high

THE REWARDS OF COMMITMENT

Commitment is costly. Expect to pay a price in

- *Hard work*—to provide the blessing to another person
- *Time*—to meaningfully touch and hug those we bless
- *Courage*—to put into a spoken message those words of love that have been on the tip of our tongue
- *Wisdom and boldness*—to highly value those we love
- *Creativity*—to picture a future for them filled with hope and with God's best for their lives.

All this effort is worthwhile. Perhaps one day, you'll see a report like Kim's, a teenager who wrote this paper for an English class.

"My parents are out to get me."

Common thinking of teenagers—I was no different. Their favorite word was "no." Their favorite saying, "You are not them." Their favorite action, grounding me.

As the years went on I gained their trust, their respect and my independence. "Yes" was almost always the reply. Compromise became an alternative. Going out with them could be fun. I was discovering freedom.

They were trying their best to raise a kid—a kid with morals, love, and goals.

Yes, my parents were out to get me—get me ready for adulthood.

Wayne and Peggy found that their determination to bless their Down's Syndrome daughter, Sarah Ann, was well worth the effort. Today, Sarah Ann is seven years old. Wayne says, "It's the best seven years of our lives. Sarah Ann is the greatest thing that ever happened to us."

The eleventh chapter of Hebrews records:

By faith Isaac blessed Jacob and Esau in regard to their future.

By faith Jacob, when he was dying, blessed each of Joseph's sons, and worshiped as he leaned on the top of his staff (vv. 20–21).

Underscore the words that show why God honored these two men in this chapter on faith.

What will God record about you? What will your children say of you? Will they be so blessed that, like the children of the woman in Proverbs 31, they will rise up and call you blessed?

Part Three

RECEIVING THE BLESSING AS AN ADULT

18

Learning to Live Without the Blessing

Healing Old Wounds

In an article in *Newsweek*, Joseph M. Queenan recalled his miserable years of growing up with an alcoholic father.[1] Three years before he wrote the article, his father, then a recovering alcoholic, came to him and apologized. He said to Queenan, "Son, I'm sorry for anything I may have done to harm you."

Queenan rejected the apology, resenting the words "may have done" and what he felt to be an almost ritualistic tendering of the apology—as if it were an assignment rather than prompted by real feeling. He had hated his father for the first twenty years of his life. He stated he didn't hate him any more because he had looked into his father's past. He discovered his father had also had an alcoholic father, that he grew up during the Depression, that he was a high school dropout, that he served an eighteen-month prison term for going AWOL to his mother's funeral, and that he had four children he couldn't support.

However, instead of feeling compassion for his father, Queenan said, "I wish him well, but I don't want to see him. I understand, but I won't forgive. It's too late to say, 'I'm sorry.'"

HOW DO WE DEAL WITH HAVING MISSED THE BLESSING?

Is it ever too late? Queenan made some good choices, some bad. He made the effort to understand his father, but he refused to forgive him. What should we do if we've missed the blessing?

The sooner we come to grips with the fact that we may never get the blessing from those who seem not to have it to give, the sooner we can turn our energies to other pursuits. We need to deal with our pain and grief and get on with our lives.

Face Up to the Problem

First, we need to examine our feelings and memories to see how much we perceived we were blessed or missed the blessing. Regardless of the fact, the perception of having been blessed or not blessed is the reality we feel.

Answering the following questions will help you determine how much you felt you were blessed.

What family members should have given you the blessing? List as many as you feel were responsible to accept and love you.

_____

_____

_____

How much blessing did you get? Mark the initials of each person you named above on the scale.

−4	−3	−2	−1	0	1	2	3	4	5	6	7	8
Abuse		Curse		Nothing		Some		Fair		Lots		All

(Remember to curse is to dishonor, to value lightly or below worth.)

How was the blessing given? Which of the eight steps of the blessing discussed so far were used or left out? (Example: *Dad never said he loved me (spoke message), but he always took me to ballgames with him.)* _____

_____

_____

_____

_____

_____

_____

Did anyone else—a teacher, coach, friend, employer—bless you in any way? Record an incident you remember.

_____

_____

_____

_____

_____

_____

Record an incident in which those responsible to bless you withheld the blessing or abused you instead.

_____

_____

_____

_____

_____

_____

_____

Though it may be painful to dredge up hurtful memories, only in facing them can we begin the healing process. For some, understanding why they feel as they do is enough to set them on the track to healing.

Jackie wrote, "I felt once again totally rejected and went through a period of depression. Eventually, I just gave all of my grief to my heavenly Father. That is, until I read *The Blessing* and discovered my underlying problem. I can now begin to go about my life with the understanding of my search for the blessing. I want more than anything to break the chain and to bless my children."

How have you reacted to a lack of blessing? Check any statements that apply to you.

1. _____ I feel that I just exist, my life is not significant.
2. _____ I'm afraid of being disloyal and so hold my hurt inside, refusing to admit it.
3. _____ Most relationships in my life are negative.
4. _____ I have a deep sense of inferiority.
5. _____ I'm angry, like Queenan, and refuse to forgive.
6. _____ Like my parents, I did not give my children the blessing, so I've messed up their lives, too.
7. _____ I usually give my kids what I wanted and didn't get.
8. _____ I hope my spouse, my job, my possessions, or a move to a new place will fill the gap I sense in my heart.
9. _____ I expect God to supply my needs.

Which of these responses do you think are positive and lead to healing?

_____

Which will only dig you deeper into lack of self-esteem and anger?

_____

Based on your replies to the above exercise, how much healing do you think needs to be done in your life?

_____

_____

_____

The next step toward healing is to discover, as Queenan did, why your parents were unable or unwilling to give you the blessing.

Understand Your Parents' Background

Part of the healing process comes when we know why our parents acted the way they did. Queenan discovered several mitigating facts about his father that explained why he did what he did. We need to do the same thing.

Begin searching out your parents' history. Find and call or write your aunts and uncles. Ask them questions about your mother's or father's childhood. Record what you find out here. _____

_____

_____

_____

_____

_____

_____

_____

_____

_____

_____

_____

Look through old family photo albums to see what information you can glean about your parents. What do you see?

_____

_____

_____

_____

_____

Did anyone in the family keep journals? Ask those who do if they are willing to share their journal with you. Record what you find about your parents.

_____

_____

_____

_____

Did your father or mother keep a journal? Ask them if you may read through their life story. What do they say that is revealing? How does the information you've uncovered help you to understand why your father or mother acted as they did?

_____

_____

_____

_____

_____

For you whose parent or parents died before you were old enough to remember them, the following assignment may help you feel their blessing.

First, complete the history project we just walked through. Find out everything you can about what kind of person your mother or father was.

As you do your research, take pictures of your parent's home, the schools he or she went to, his or her family members who are still living, places he or she probably visited like the local theater or baseball diamond. Put together a photo album that reflects what his or her life was like, annotated with comments from relatives and friends.

Then, visit your parent's grave. Take pictures of the headstone or marker and the surroundings. Perhaps have someone take a picture of you standing by the headstone.

Finally, write yourself a letter of blessing from that parent, using the information you've gleaned. Write it as you honestly think he or she might have given you the blessing had he or she lived. You can use the space below to write and then copy it and include it in your album.

_____

_____

_____

_____

_____

_____

_____

_____

_____

_____

_____

_____

_____

Forgive Our Parents

Our healing is dependent on our willingness to forgive those who have hurt us. If you, like Queenan, choose not to forgive, then you'll spend the rest of your life fighting the results of having missed the blessing. Healing cannot take place. On the other hand, if you forgive, the hurt feelings can be put behind, and you can find a fulfilling life.

In our book the *Gift of Honor*, we share the story of Denny, an angry young man who threw his abusive father out a second story window! He eventually came to forgive his father and even had the joy of leading him to Christ. He also had the joy of seeing most of his family forgive his father and find freedom—all but one sister.

After Denny had taken his father to her home to ask forgiveness, she wrote:

> Father, your coming to see me was an outrage! There is no way you can come and preach forgiveness to me after all the scars I bear from you. For years, you have been all I have thought about. My every word, each decision I have made.
>
> You have been responsible for my becoming a prostitute. You are responsible for my marriage that broke up. You are the reason I have had an operation so I can never have children—I'm afraid of what I'd do to them. You ask me to forgive you? You are not to be forgiven. You are to be conquered. If it takes me the rest of my life, I'll bury your memory. Don't ever call or come to see me again.

What happened? Denny is free and at peace, but his sister's life has been controlled by hatred and bitterness for years because she made a decision out of her hurt to treat others with as little value as she herself received. She devalues God. She is blind to how much God values her. She dishonors her father's memory, and she remains in emotional and spiritual chains.

Healing comes with forgiveness. The following Bible verses deal with forgiveness. Underscore or highlight the words that reveal God's standard of forgiveness, then write, in your own words, what the verse says about your need to forgive others. The first verse is done as a sample for you to follow.

"For *if you forgive* men when they sin against you, *your heavenly Father will also forgive you*" (Matt. 6:14 [italics added for emphasis]).

(My forgiveness from God depends on my forgiving others.)

_____

_____

_____

"Then Peter came to Jesus and asked, 'Lord, how many times shall I forgive my brother [father, mother] when he sins against me? Up to seven times?'

Jesus answered, 'I tell you, not seven times, but seventy-seven times [or seventy times seven]" (Matt. 18:21–22).

_____

_____

_____

_____

"And when you stand praying, if you hold anything against anyone, forgive him, so that your Father in heaven may forgive you your sins" (Mark 11:25).

_____

_____

_____

_____

"Be kind and compassionate to one another, forgiving each other, just as in Christ God forgave you" (Eph. 4:32).

_____

_____

_____

"Bear with each other and forgive whatever grievances you may have against one another. Forgive as the Lord forgave you" (Col. 3:13).

_____

_____

_____

Forgiveness, like love, is a decision we make. It's not impossible if we pray for God's enabling and determine we're going to do it. It will most likely be painful, for forgiveness is accepting the hurt that was given and freeing the one who hurt us from all blame.

List, in order of difficulty, the things you find the hardest to forgive. (Change the headings to other persons who had responsibility for raising you if you didn't know either your father or mother.)

Mother	Father

Why are these things so difficult to forgive? _____

_____

_____

_____

_____

_____

_____

If you have sisters or brothers who also feel the lack of blessing, ask them what is most difficult for them to forgive and why. How do their answers compare with yours?

_____

_____

_____

_____

_____

_____

_____

What have you decided about forgiving your father or mother?

_____

If your parents are living, how will you contact them to talk with them to tell them you forgive them? _____

_____

_____

_____

_____

_____

Write out what you need to say.

Father, _____

_____

_____

_____

_____

_____

_____

_____

Mother, _____

_____

_____

_____

_____

_____

_____

_____

When will you do this? _____

If your parents are no longer living, use the space above to write out your statement of forgiveness anyway. Give a copy to your spouse or a friend to read. This will give you a feeling of having completed the task.

Why is forgiving your parents so important? Highlight the answer in the following verses:

"Each of you must respect his mother and father . . . I am the LORD your God" (Lev. 19:3).

"Cursed is the man who dishonors his father or his mother" (Deut. 27:16).

"For God said, 'Honor your father and mother' and 'Anyone who curses his father or mother must be put to death'" (Matt. 15:4).

"'Honor your father and mother'—which is the first commandment with a promise—'that it may go well with you and that you may enjoy long life on the earth'" (Eph. 6:2).

HONORING OUR PARENTS

Forgiving is the first step in honoring our parents. But it is only the first step. We must go on to give them the honor that God demands.

Circle **T** or **F** beside the following statements:

T or **F**   On a scale of 1 to 100, I value my mother at 50 or below.

T or **F**   One a scale of 1 to 100, I value my father at 50 or below.

T or **F**   I keep my parent(s) at arm's length, never letting them get close to me emotionally.

T or **F**   I don't pay much attention to what my parent(s) says.

T or **F**   I never discuss issues that matter with my parent(s), only small talk.

T or **F**   I let weeks and months go by without seeking out my parent(s).

T or **F**   I never talk to my parent(s) about the hurts I felt as a child.

T or **F**   I feel anger bubbling just below the surface any time I am with my parent(s), but never express it.

T or **F**   I often say negative things about my parent(s) to my spouse or children.

T or **F**   I blame my parent(s) for failures in my life.

T or **F**   I'd be glad if something awful happened to my parent(s).

How many of the statements did you mark true? _____

Even one true statement indicates that you hold your parents in lower esteem than is God's standard. Proverbs 20:20 states, "If a man curses his father or mother,/his lamp will be snuffed out in pitch darkness."

Though our dishonoring actions may cause pain to our parents, they cause far deeper, longer lasting problems for us. They keep us from being free to be the people God designed us to be.

To help you give honor to your parents, write down one specific incident of their withholding the blessing that makes you angriest or hurts the most, one you remember most vividly.

_____

_____

_____

_____

_____

_____

_____

In what ways has this incident increased your awareness of others' needs and pain? _____

_____

_____

_____

_____

What benefits, if any, can you see that have come from this incident? _____

_____

_____

_____

Has this incident drawn members of your family together? If so, how? _____

_____

_____

_____

How has this incident drawn you closer to God's love?

_____

_____

_____

_____

Review the past six questions and note the benefits you derived from this incident, despite how awful it was when it happened.

_____

_____

_____

_____

_____

What insights does this exercise give you about honoring your parents? (Example: Even though what they did hurt terribly, in the long run, I learned much from what happened to me and that good did come from the bad.) _____

_____

_____

_____

_____

_____

_____

How does this make you feel about giving honor to your parents?

_____

_____

What would it take to change your true answers to false so you could honor your parents?

_____

_____

_____

_____

_____

When will you begin? _____

We need to begin now, but don't expect the process to be over in a day or two. Healing may take months, even years, to complete. We weren't hurt in a single instant, and neither will healing happen that fast.

If your hurts are deep, like those of Denny's sister, you may need to go beyond the scope of this workbook and seek professional counseling. In Proverbs 1:5, it is written, "A wise man will hear and increase in learning,/and a man of understanding will acquire wise counsel" (NASB). Don't let anything keep you from doing what is necessary to find the healing you need.

CHANGING A CURSE TO A BLESSING

Earlier, we defined a curse as valuing lightly, below actual worth, to dishonor or despise. If your perception of your parents is that they dishonored you, three Bible verses may help you on the way to healing.

Underscore meaningful words in the following verses.

"However, the LORD your God would not listen to Balaam but turned the curse into a blessing for you, because the LORD your God loves you" (Deut. 23:5).

"It may be that the LORD will see my distress and repay me with good for the cursing I am receiving today" (2 Sam. 16:12).

"Like a fluttering sparrow or a darting swallow, an undeserved curse does not come to rest" (Prov. 26:2).

These verses lead us to the next step and the next chapter: turning to God's family blessing.

19

Receiving God's Blessing

Becoming a Child of God

The blessing began with God. You'll remember from Chapter 3 that the first thing God did after creating Adam and Eve was to bless them. The blessing comes full circle and ends with God.

A person who includes God in his or her life can walk through all eight elements of the blessing: evaluating the blessing, giving meaningful touch, speaking words of blessing, expressing high value and a special future, committing to seeing the blessing through, learning to live without the blessing, and receiving God's family blessing.

In fact, we feel strongly that no one can know the *full measure* of the blessing unless they have a personal relationship with Jesus Christ. Without the blessing that comes directly from our heavenly Father to His children, even a full parental blessing can't quite fill our cup.

Those who didn't receive the blessing from their parents can get it in its entirety from God—if they are children of God.

Those who missed the blessing and had a portion of it supplied by a spouse or friend or child (remember, these can supply only about 80 percent) can fill their cup to the brim with God's blessing—if they are children of God.

Contrary to popular belief, not every person created by God is a member of God's family. How, then, does one become a child of God? Highlight the words in the following verses as suggested.

"Yet to all who received him, to those who believed in his name, he gave the right to become children of God" (John 1:12).

"And without faith it is impossible to please God, because anyone who comes to him must believe that he exists and that he rewards those who earnestly seek him" (Heb. 11:6).

Why is belief necessary? Romans 3:23 gives the answer. "For all have sinned and fall short of the glory of God."

What is the penalty for non-belief? "Whoever believes in him is not condemned, but whoever does not believe stands condemned already because he has not believed in the name of God's one and only Son" (John 3:18).

The judgment for sin is found in Ezekiel 18:4. "For every living soul belongs to me, the father as well as the son—both alike belong to me. The soul who sins is the one who will die." The same judgment is seen in Romans 6:23: "For the wages of sin is death."

In John 5:24, the blessing given to those who believe is, "I tell you the truth, whoever hears my word and believes him who sent me has eternal life and will not be condemned; he has crossed over from death to life."

The blessing of life is given freely. Romans 5:8: "But God demonstrates his own love for us in this: While we were still sinners, Christ died for us."

Not only does God's blessing mean eternal life for His children, it gives much more. What else do we receive according to Matthew 6:33? "But seek first his kingdom and his righteousness, and all these things will be given to you as well."

This promise is backed with another in Philippians 4:19: "And my God will meet all your needs according to his glorious riches in Christ Jesus."

Have you believed in Jesus' name and received Him?

If you have not and want to be sure of receiving all the blessing God has to give (and we've mentioned only a mere smattering), now is the time to do so.

Simply talk to God, admit to Him that you have sinned, ask His forgiveness, and tell Him you want to accept the sacrifice for sin that Jesus offered for you. Tell Him you want the blessing of eternal life that Jesus offers. Jesus promised, "whoever comes to me I will never drive away" (John 6:37).

Ask God to direct you to a person who can help you to learn how to receive all the blessing God has to give. A pastor in your area who preaches from the Bible should be able to lead you into the next steps of the Christian life. If you know of no one, please write to us at Today's Family, P.O. Box 22111, Phoenix, AZ 85028.

When we have a personal relationship with Jesus Christ, God Himself becomes our Father and blesses us with every spiritual blessing in Christ Jesus.

How secure is our relationship according to this verse? "I give them eternal life, and they shall never perish; no one can snatch them out of my hand. My Father, who has given them to me, is greater than all; no one can snatch them out of my Father's hand" (John 10:28–29).

_____

_____

_____

What additional promise of security do you find in the following statement? "I am convinced that neither death nor life, neither angels nor demons, neither the present nor the future, nor any powers, neither height nor depth, nor anything else in all creation, will be able to separate us from the love of God that is in Christ Jesus our Lord" (Rom. 8:38–39).

_____

_____

_____

The Bible describes Jesus Christ as "the same yesterday and to-day and forever" (Heb. 13:18). How does this information add to the security of our relationship with our heavenly Father?

_____

_____

The secret of getting the blessing from God is expecting a blessing from Him only. Have you been looking for the blessing from any of the following?

_____ Parents
_____ Other family members
_____ Spouse
_____ Children
_____ Moving to a new location
_____ Getting more and better possessions
_____ Having a bigger, newer home
_____ Being promoted into a better job
_____ Gaining recognition in your community

How well have any of these worked in making you feel completely blessed? _____

Instead of looking to any of these or other similar people, places, possessions, or positions to give us the blessing, we simply ask God for His direct blessing.

The following are guidelines—not a magic formula—to seeking God's blessings:

1. Confess to God that you've been looking for the blessing in all the wrong places.

What do you need to say to Him? _____

_____

_____

_____

_____

2. Recognize that only God can fill you with the blessing and that temptation to find it elsewhere is empty.

What do you need that only God can fill? _____

_____

_____

_____

_____

3. Rejoice in the relationship you have with God. Thank Him joyfully for all the blessings He has to give.

What has God done in your life that gives you cause to rejoice?

_____

_____

_____

_____

_____

4. Make God your best friend. Spend time with Him: just communing with Him, reading the Bible, praying, praising, singing, doing those things that develop friendships between two people.

How much time do you spend each day getting to know God?

_____

What will you do with God on a daily basis? _____

_____

_____

_____

_____

5. Decide to be blessed. Don't be impatient, but rest in God's faithfulness and the knowledge that He will do the best for you at the right time. Be grateful and content with what He gives.

How long have you waited for God to answer your request to be filled? _____

Why have you given up? _____

_____

How much longer would you be willing to wait? _____

_____

_____

God has promised to be our rock, shield, rear guard, shepherd, rescuer, hiding place, living water, bread of life, light, advocate, eternal abundant life, and our source of wisdom, joy, peace, love, and blessing—just for starters. What He has promised, He will do. All we have to do is ask and He supplies.

Having a heavenly Father who will always love us and care for us is in itself awesome, but it is not all.

OUR SPIRITUAL FAMILY

In addition to His own blessing, God provides a spiritual family—other believers who become like brothers and sisters, fathers and mothers, aunts and uncles. These people are available to help meet our needs. God knows our need for meaningful touch and for the physical companionship of others to build up our lives and encourage us, and this is the way he has chosen to provide.

Fae, like many others, received the elements of the blessing from a spiritual "mother." She says, "God has given me at least one person in my life who has blessed me. Neither of my parents ever gave me or my brothers the family blessing. I grew up hurting.

"Then I met a Sunday school teacher. Although my mother never went to church, she allowed me to go to Sunday school with a neighbor girl. I'd only gone a couple of weeks, so I was surprised when Miss Joscelyn's eyes lit up when I walked into the room that third week. She began giving me hugs each Sunday, and she'd ask about how my week had been. She was like a spiritual mother to me and made a tremendous difference in my life. I'll never forget her."

Who from God's spiritual family has entered your life to bless you as the Sunday school teacher did Fae?

_____

How did you meet? _____

_____

_____

What has he or she done? _____

_____

_____

_____

_____

What has been the result in your life? _____

_____

_____

_____

_____

If you could choose a spiritual sister, brother, mother, or father, what qualifications would you look for?

_____

_____

_____

_____

_____

Where do you meet a spiritual family member to bless you? Try one of the following places.

_____ A Sunday school class
_____ A church singles group, if you're single
_____ A Wednesday evening service (usually smaller than Sunday mornings)
_____ A men's or women's group in the church
_____ Other? _____

Whether or not you have been blessed by a spiritual sister or brother, have you considered blessing others? _____

_____

Who might you choose from your spiritual family to bless? _____

_____

_____

Why would you choose that person? _____

_____

_____

_____

What could you do to bless him or her? _____

_____

_____

_____

_____

One woman attending a large church decided to help others in the spiritual family to give at least a part of the blessing. She designed a form like the one following:

Name _____

I saw Jesus in you today when you:

_____

_____

_____

_____

_____

She made copies on half sheets of pastel paper and made them available to everyone in her church. Anyone can pick up a supply, fill them out, and give or send them to the ones he or she wants to bless.

They're very effective. Jan used one to express the blessing she'd felt from a new business acquaintance. The woman responded with a note to say that the message was just what she needed to lift her spirits after a particularly difficult day.

What could you do as an individual to bless others in the family of God? _____

_____

_____

_____

_____

CHURCHES THAT GIVE THE BLESSING

Sometimes an individual Christian reaches out to bless another. Sometimes a whole church gets involved and works at blessing everyone the congregation can reach.

Overlake Christian Church in Kirkland, Washington—just across Lake Washington from Seattle—is such a church. On a large scale, the church provides fellowship groups that consist of twelve to twenty people. Each group studies the Bible together as part of its weekly meeting, but the members also give the blessing to each another.

One group had a golden opportunity to bless. Brad and Shirley were members of the group. One afternoon, Shirley arrived home from grocery shopping with their two little girls and found Brad dead in his study. The first person she called was the leader of her fellowship group.

Individual members of the group came to her aid: some took care of notifying authorities; others provided food; some made the necessary arrangements; some took care of the little girls for several weeks; some provided money to take care of current bills; one man did mechanical work on her car so she'd have dependable transportation; all prayed with Shirley and spent time comforting her.

In the midst of the worst tragedy of Shirley's life, she felt loved and cared for by her spiritual family.

What blessing vehicle is available at your church?

_____

_____

_____

_____

_____

Another church provides blessing cards that individuals can use these to give a message of high esteem to others. These 3x5 cards are kept in the pew pockets. People are encouraged to fill them out and drop them in the offering plate. The church office sees that they are mailed to the right person.

These cards make it simpler to bless another, but you don't need a form to write a blessing to someone. You can use a notecard or stationery. Choose a person you know in God's spiritual family. Ask God to enable you to recognize whom He's leading you to bless:

_____ A widow whose children live in another state

_____ A single parent who needs a lift

_____ A newcomer that hasn't made friends yet

_____ The man or woman who's "different"

_____ The family who's always late for church

_____ The organist who never misses a Sunday

_____ The pastor, who probably seldom hears of blessing

_____ Your choice _____

Write a note of blessing that includes expression of high value or a special future for that person. We've left room for you to do practice drafts for two people. _____

_____

_____

_____

_____

_____

_____

_____

_____

_____

Overlake Christian Church has yet another way of giving the blessing. The Deaconess Program has an outreach called the Encouragers. They send appropriate cards to anyone brought to their attention who is hurting: those suffering a loss, an illness, any kind of hurtful occasion, when a word from a spiritual friend brings comfort.

You, too, could send greeting cards to bless others. Think of different occasions, like birthdays, when you could give a word of esteem or promise:

_____   _____

_____   _____

_____   _____

_____   _____

_____   _____

_____   _____

The Grace Bible Church in Bozeman, Montana, has a program within its elementary Christian Education program to bless children from grades one through five. They call it the Pal program.

Any child in that age group can request a Pal. To do so the child fills out a form, giving his or her interests and other information. Adults in the congregation, ranging in age from college students to grandparents, volunteer to be Pals to the children. They must first apply with the administrator of the program, who determines the qualifications of the persons to be Pals. Qualifications include 1) accepting Jesus Christ as Savior; 2) being known personally by someone in church leadership; 3) leading a Christian walk worth following.

The adult Pals also fill out an interest form similar to the one the child fills out. This is given to the youngster when a match is made.

The coordinator then matches children and adults with like interests, so they can enjoy activities together.

Generally, the coordinator asks the parents of the child to invite the Pals for coffee or a meal to get acquainted. When the child and his/her parents feel comfortable with the Pal, the Pal can take the child out for whatever activities both enjoy.

The program requires that Pals make contact at least once a month, more often if possible. Either the Pal or the child can initiate a meeting. The Christian Education department at Grace Bible Church produces two or three programs a year that the child can invite the Pal to attend.

Does it work? "Yes!" says the coordinator. One child asked for a grandmother-aged person. The woman chosen was a widow with no family in the community. She invited her youngster to various activities, and the child invited the grandmother to music recitals. Before long, the family began asking the grandmother to holiday dinners. The child got wonderful affirmation and blessing from the older adult; the older adult found a new spiritual family to fill many vacant hours.

In yet another incident, a young boy was paired with a college student. The college student not only befriended the young boy, but also the whole family, running errands and doing odd jobs. Before long, the college student was invited to live with them and become an integral part of the family.

If a pairing of adult and child doesn't click, the coordinator can replace the adult with another. During the first two years of the program, more children asked for Pals than adults volunteered. But in the third year, more adults signed up to be Pals. They'd heard of the great blessing it is to work one-on-one with a child.

If you'd like to start a Pal program in your church, you can begin with the forms shown. For more information, contact the Grace Bible Church at 8 West Olive Street, Bozeman, MT 59715.

What church do you know of that makes a point of giving the blessing? (Please write and tell us your church's "blessing" story. We'd love to hear it!) _____

What does that church do? _____

_____

_____

_____

_____

_____

What does your church do? _____

_____

_____

_____

_____

_____

How could you be a spark that ignites your church into giving the blessing? _____

_____

_____

_____

_____

_____

We come to the end of our journey together. It is our sincere prayer that in working through this workbook, you have found blessing in learning to give meaningful touch, a spoken message of high value and special future, and have committed yourself to bless those God has given you to bless.

We pray that you have gained the blessing for yourself, that you have strengthened the bonds of your family and friendships by giving each one a full portion of the blessing, and that you are reaching out to members of God's family to bless them.

May God bless you and keep you, and may His face always shine upon you.

Notes

Chapter 2
1. Peterson and Bossio, *Health and Optimism* (Free Press).
2. *USA Today*

Chapter 8
1. Andor Foldes, "Beethoven's Kiss."
2. Dolores Krieger, "Therapeutic Touch: The Imprimatur of Nursing," *American Journal of Nursing*, May 1975, 784.
3. Diane Ackerman, *A Natural History of the Senses* (New York: Random House, 1990.)
4. Judith Hooper, "The Hug Factor," *Health*, October 1989, 73.
5. *Ibid*, 74.
6. Helen Colton, *The Gift of Touch* (New York: Seaview/Putnam, 1983), 102.
7. Marc H. Hollender, "The Wish to Be Held," *Archives of General Psychiatry*, vol. 22, 1970, 446.
8. Ross Campbell, *How to Really Love Your Child* (Wheaton: Victor Books, 1977), 73.

Chapter 10
1. Dotson Rader, "What Loves Means," *Parade*, March 8, 1992, 4.

Chapter 11
1. E. Pollinger, copyright © 1990. Used by permission.

Chapter 15
1. William Glasser, *Control Theory* (San Francisco: Harper Collins, · 1985), 19.
2. Toni Mack, "My Father Said I Was Stupid," *Forbes*, September 2, 1992, 98.

Chapter 18
1. Joseph M. Queenan, "Too Late to Say, 'I'm Sorry'," *Newsweek*, August 31, 1987, 7.